# YOUR
# FIRST
# JOB

# YOUR
# FIRST
# JOB

Choosing, getting and keeping it

## VIVIEN DONALD AND RAY GROSE

KOGAN
PAGE

First published in 1984, written by Anne Page.
Second edition 1993, written by Vivien Donald and Ray Grose (who has incorporated material from his previously published work).
Third edition 1997

Kogan Page Limited
120 Pentonville Road
London N1 9JN

© Kogan Page 1984
© Kogan Page and RW Grose 1993, 1997

**British Library Cataloguing in Publication Data**

A CIP record for this book is available from the British Library.

ISBN 0–7494–2150–9

Typeset by DP Photosetting, Aylesbury, Bucks
Printed and bound in Great Britain by
Clays Ltd, St Ives plc

# Contents

# Introduction

One of the most important decisions of your life is the choice of your first job. Your initial employment is likely to set the foundation of your entire career. It may influence who will be your friends, even whom you will marry. It could determine your total life experience.

The choice of your first job is probably the most complex and critical decision that you will have to face at this stage in your life. Because of its importance and potentially far-reaching consequences, this decision demands maximum effort to ensure the best possible outcome. Your input will require searching assessment of your personality, desires and ambitions to a depth to which you are unlikely to have gone before.

A 'good' job is the number one priority for most young people. They want a job that will be interesting and satisfying, and hope that it will offer them personal growth and social development. A good job should also provide the financial base on which to build a career and develop 'quality' in their lives.

However, youth unemployment suggests that good jobs are becoming harder to find and that competition for them is increasing. In this competitive environment the young job seeker and the new employee need all the help they can get. This book will provide practical recommendations that will add 'value' to the job seeker/new employee in the eyes of the employer, and this 'value' will be the help up the ladder needed in these difficult times.

This book will show you how to choose and get the job best

suited to you. It will then explain what must be done in the early stages to keep the job – something which few new employees know. Finally, it will describe what should be done to be successful in the longer term.

There are three major recurring concepts in this book which are fundamental to achievement in the workplace:

- The first is the importance of developing a personal image, appropriate to the particular organisation, and then 'selling' it.
- The second is that this image is dependent upon the quality and extent of relationships that the employee is able to develop and sustain.
- Finally, it is essential to develop habits in setting personal and work-related objectives and to plan in a disciplined manner how to achieve them.

The suggestions and concepts covered here apply equally to school and college leavers and university graduates. They are appropriate to positions in government or private industry. While the emphasis is on new job situations, the concepts depicted relate to many recurrent work circumstances that occur during the learning and challenging experience of a working life. In this respect the book will be a valuable reference guide throughout any chosen career.

# Chapter 1

# Career-led Choices at School

During your first three years at secondary school you will have followed a broad-based range of subjects, mainly studied separately, though possibly some were taken together in an integrated programme. The course will have stretched across the curriculum from 'arts' subjects such as English, history, geography and probably one or two modern languages, through 'practical' subjects like home economics, design, technology, art and music, to maths and sciences. You will also have spent time on games and physical education, and religious studies.

Secondary schools in this country almost all agree that most young people cannot continue to study all these subjects right through to GCSE level. When you are about 14, at Key Stage 4, you will begin to think about choosing which of them you will study more deeply, ready for GCSEs.

The choice cannot be entirely free for each student since there might not be enough teachers to go round if everyone made a different choice. Most schools, therefore, offer blocks of subjects from which you can select the subjects you prefer. The idea is to try to provide those who know exactly what they want with the chance to decide, while making sure that those who are not yet certain still have the broadest possible base and flexibility.

Your careers lessons or guidance at school will make you look at your strong and weak points, and to relate these to subject choices, and even to possible future jobs. Your teachers will provide information about each subject and what is involved if you take it up. They will tell you which examinations follow from various courses. Careers materials give you information about particular job and/or course requirements, and teachers who know you especially well – such as your form tutor, or your head of year or house – will help you sort out what might be best suited to you personally. Most schools arrange an evening display designed to help you and your parents together understand what is on offer for the following years. Your parents will no doubt have ideas for you, too, which may not be all bad!

At this stage, it is obviously important not to miss out on a subject that may later prove crucial to your study or job, but on the other hand, there can be a danger in thinking that 'it's now or never'. If you take up areas you find later to be of little interest, it will rarely stop you changing course.

Don't forget that few types of work stay the same for ever and the best equipped person is one who can be flexible, and who is able to cope with new ideas and adapt to the technologies of the future. So, your best bet is to choose a balance of subjects, leaving your options open and ensuring that you have a good education for life in general, and that you do rewarding work for your next two years in school. Here are some hints for doing just that:

- Be aware of your own strengths and weaknesses and choose subjects you are good at, and find pleasure in studying.
- Ask teachers, tutors, other staff and older pupils what particular courses are like.
- Look at the work involved in each subject and maker sure that you select a variety of practical and academic subjects.
- Allow yourself to take some subjects because you like them, and not necessarily just because you need them. Never choose a subject just because your friends are taking it.
- If you have an idea at this stage about the particular type of work you would like to do later, make sure that you are following the right subjects for it.

So, the key to a well-planned choice of subjects is balance. This is not too difficult to achieve since certain subjects are compulsory, and you can choose between a range of other non-compulsory subjects and possibly decide on some extra, or slightly unusual, subjects, according to your taste.

## Compulsory subjects

English, maths, science, design and technology, modern foreign languages, and information technology prepare you well for the outside world. Not only will employers and further and higher education establishments want to know about your proficiency in English and maths, but you will also need to be at least competent in those subjects to get the most from your adult role later. There are very few areas of work – or play – in which you would find no computers in use, and so information technology has become an invaluable compulsory subject. Your school may teach this as a separate subject, or teach it alongside others where computers are used.

The school probably offers a double science course, or even all three separate sciences, although only one is compulsory; again, science is so often needed for further education courses that the further you can continue with extra sciences, the better.

In both design and technology and modern foreign languages, you may be able to study for GCSE Short Course qualifications. This also applies to physical education, which is a compulsory subject.

## Non-compulsory subjects

You can gain GCSE Short Course qualifications in non-compulsory subjects, too, such as art, music, history and geography. Pupils aged 14, at Key Stage 4, can drop non-compulsory subjects like art and music, and either choose between history and geography or take a short course in both, depending on which GCSE subjects are being taken. The subjects roughly fall into two groups: humanities and science.

# Humanities

*English literature.* If you are interested in reading and analysing novels, plays and poems you should take English literature in addition to English language. The idea is to increase your knowledge and add to your enjoyment of literature. Moreover, you will find that many types of work involve a sound knowledge of English literature though they may not actually require it: work in the theatre, journalism, broadcasting and teaching, for example.

*Geography.* The aim here is to give you an understanding of the environment and communities – local, national and world-wide – in which you live. You can study through work in the field – that is, outside the classroom – as well as at school, and be able to take GCSE and A level. Geography could play a useful part in: mining, geology, surveying, farming and town-planning.

*History.* This subject involves asking fundamental questions such as: Why did that happen? How do we know that happened? What happened as a result of that event? What does it all mean for us today? You search for evidence and clues about events and people in the past, which means doing personal research as well as a great deal of reading and writing. All sorts of jobs require a knowledge of history, either in itself, like archaeological work or restoring paintings, or for what it tells us about the world as it is now; history is, for instance, of great use to diplomats and economists.

*Modern languages.* All secondary schools offer the chance to study at least one modern foreign language, and some far more than that. In certain areas where the languages spoken at home are numerous and not only European, the schools allow individual young people or very small groups to study their mother tongue for exam purposes. It is obviously useful to leave school with a knowledge of other languages and of how other people live: it may help you to find work, be useful in further study where relevant tests are written in different languages, or it may simply make things easier for you when you have the chance to travel abroad.

Remember that many higher education courses – ie those taken at a college or university – require a language GCSE, so if you already know what you want to do at that level, check the language requirement now. If languages are not your strong point, and you find yourself bored by German and unhappy with French, you may be better off taking another subject more to your taste now, and picking up languages at evening classes or special crash courses later if you find you really need them. (There is nothing like having a real motivation to learn a language fast!)

## The sciences

The division of sciences into specialised subjects is an artificial and increasingly old-fashioned one. In reality the separate sciences overlap and use similar methods. That is why in many schools you will have followed an integrated science course in your first three years. Most people can take a combined science course leading to a double GCSE, but some can take a simple science, to allow more time to work on other subjects. Or the school may offer a course in biology, chemistry and physics, all of which have to be taken to GCSE level. You will find it an advantage if you are also good at mathematics. This is true for all science subjects but especially physics at GCSE level.

*Physics.* This will be virtually indispensable for any future work in the scientific or technical worlds. It is the study of light, heat, magnetism, electricity, electronics, sound, radioactivity and mechanical energy, together with that of the properties of matter. If you are interested in knowing more about the world around you from a scientific point of view – what causes a rainbow? Can we get useful energy from sea waves and the wind? – and if you are thinking of becoming an engineer, electrician, optician, astronomer, laboratory technician, pilot, metallurgist or geologist, for example, then this will be your choice.

*Biology.* This is the study of living things. You will learn about the structure of plants and animals – what they are made of and how they work – in their natural environment. You need to be quite literate to choose biology as you will have to acquire a whole new vocabulary of specialised names and descriptive terms. It is wise to think of taking chemistry along with biology, especially if you want to go on to further study.

*Chemistry.* Key Stage 4 courses cover all aspects of chemistry, including the study of elements, chemical compounds, reactions, gases, inorganic and organic chemistry. The subject is highly practical and, for work in the laboratory, you will need to show great patience and care. You will get a good base for further study in bio-chemistry, pharmacology, beauty therapy, or hairdressing, for example.

# Practical subjects

*Home economics.* Courses in home economics include practical subjects such as textiles, food, or child development. They will teach you many skills which will be useful to you, whether or not you follow a career based on any of them.

*Design and technology.* Here you may follow courses requiring you to use a computer to plan and think about a design, then to make a model and test it. If you follow graphic communication you will not only be able to understand and produce drawings from which objects could be made, but you will also learn how to present information visually so that others can understand it. You may have to design and make such electronic equipment as amplifiers and sensors, mechanisms like gears and linkages, and structures of all kinds.

*Art.* This subject develops your visual awareness and provides you with opportunities to express yourself through such activities as painting, drawing, collage, illustration and graphic design, printmaking, textiles, pottery and sculpture. A qualification in art is important for any job which is concerned with the appearance of things, such as, for example, architecture, book illustration, poster or fashion design, newspaper, book or magazine layout.

# Other subjects

There are, of course, many other possibilities open to you through short courses in Key Stage 4 such as music, drama, statistics or physical education. The choice of one or all of them is obviously helpful to certain careers of a specialised nature: music would be essential for anyone serious about a performing career, but taken in combination with physics or electronics, it could also be a valuable base for work in the recording and broadcasting industries.

This group of subjects is also related to the non-professional side of your future life, that is, time you will spend for fun, leisure and recreation. Amateur music-making and drama are age-old pleasures; taking part in sporting activity, whether in teams or individually, is both healthy and entertaining. Most schools can give you a broad range of experiences so that you can find an activity that suits you personally – judo, gymnastics and canoeing can be just as satisfying, if not more so, as the time-honoured football and hockey-type field sports, for example.

# Qualifications

A great deal of the work you do during key stage 4 will be aimed at getting you through GCSEs. You (and your teacher) may deplore the fact that you cannot study as the interest grabs you, and that you are constrained by a schedule largely determined by the examining boards. However, the fact remains that for employers and institutions of higher education your success in GCSEs, AS/A levels and GNVQs gives some indication of your intellectual and academic capacity, shows that you have the ability to learn and concentrate and also means that you know something about a specific topic.

Despite this, employers regularly point out that such things as attitudes to work, the capacity to think logically and to remember and the ability to get on with people are as important to them as proficiency in arithmetic or history.

Some qualifications that lead straight into the world of work, such as RSA exams and GNVQs, can be taken at school or after you have started work. The opportunities for adding to your qualifications through full-time or part-time study are described in the next chapter.

# Chapter 2

# Work Experience and Further Qualifications

Preparing yourself for a job while you are still at school isn't only a matter of studying and taking exams. You can also learn a great deal by doing various casual jobs – and some of them might even earn you some useful cash. However, earning money – itself an educational business – should not be the prime purpose when looking for work while still at school. The important thing is to be able to show employers, at some stage in the future, either that you have always been keen on the particular line of work they are in, or at any rate that you are reliable, capable of sustained effort and trustworthy. On the other hand, you should never take on too much, as this would make you tired and unable to concentrate on ordinary school and homework.

If you can persuade an employer not just to use you for cheap labour, but also to teach you something about the business, all the better. This is, of course, easier for the greengrocer who takes you on for Saturday sales work, than for the neighbour who offers you occasional babysitting!

You must bear in mind that your local education authority is required under the law relating to child employment to issue bylaws in respect of the amount of time you may work for money in someone else's employ. In any case, this is only permitted if you are over 13 years old, and anyone who takes you on for paid work should be aware of what the bylaws say. If you earn enough money, you will be subject to tax, just like everyone else!

Now, let us look at various types of work which you might be able to do while still at school.

# Jobs out of school

In most neighbourhoods there are possibilities for jobs that can be done part time, either in the evenings, at weekends, or during school holidays. These include:

*Babysitting.* Many parents with young children need help looking after them, for a whole host of reasons: they may have to go out to work but be unable either to come home in time to fetch their children from school in the afternoon or to stay at home with them during school holidays; they may want time to themselves while at home, to work, study or do household duties; they may want to go out at fixed times regularly for an evening class, or evening work; or they may need an occasional babysitter while they go out for an evening. People over 13 years old are legally entitled to be in charge of younger children for such purposes, and it should not be too difficult for you to find neighbours who would welcome your services in one or several of the above circumstances.

The advantages here are not only that you earn some money, but that if you are wanted when the children are still awake, you can learn useful skills both in caring for smaller people and in entertaining them. This would most certainly help you if you decided at a later stage to become a nursery nurse or a teacher. Don't forget either that even if you can't imagine anything more remote than working with young children, it may be that you will one day have some of your own and will probably be grateful for experience of children then.

*Shop assistant.* School students are often welcome part-time employees serving in shops, packing shelves or sorting materials.

In a large high-street chainstore such a job would give you an invaluable chance to see how major retailing is carried out; in a smaller shop, it would show you what the demands of a small business are.

*Paper round.* Many localities have small newsagents who offer a newspaper home delivery service. However, if you are thinking of taking on such work, you should remember that it is hard work, involving early rising, regularity and reliability.

*Cleaning.* Homes, cars and gardens constantly need cleaning, and many people welcome help with these chores. You can advertise your services by word of mouth – through your own satisfied parents, for example – or by displaying a card in a local shop.

Be prepared for hard and repetitive work, but if you stick at it you may obtain valuable character references from people who know you to be regular, trustworthy and diligent. This type of work may not necessarily be of use to you in your future career (though the office cleaning business is a fast-growing one). However, there are office and domestic cleaning agencies in most cities now which can give you work on a short-term or casual basis and this can be useful while you are looking for more satisfying jobs, or in supplementing a student grant, for instance.

## Jobs at school

There are various forms of work which relate closely to the classes you are following at school, and which may result in highly useful preparatory experience for you – and even in job offers at the end of your official school period.

*Production of publishing material.* This includes helping to produce school materials such as posters, newsletters or library catalogues.

By doing this, you may acquire a great deal of experience of design, reporting, writing, editing, printing and distribution. Most secondary schools are well-equipped with desktop publishing facilities, giving you an opportunity to become familiar with techniques and equipment that is now in use in many workplaces. School magazines and newspapers are often entered in regional and national competitions, which is one way for you to be noticed by employers who are looking for young talent in this very competitive field.

Similarly, if you find yourself in college later and want to become involved in the production of journals there, some experience at school will certainly be a help. Publishing and media jobs are generally highly sought-after, and among the many seeking work, those who have demonstrated interest and commitment in a voluntary capacity while studying, genuinely do give themselves a head start. Moreover, they are often noticed for real pieces of work they have accomplished in the student arena – news reports, scandal investigations, for example – which then find their way into the local or national media.

*Computer experience.* If your interest runs that way, you might be able to persuade teachers to let you help with some of the tasks they have to perform on the school's computer. Data about student attendance, for instance, needs collecting, recording and analysing, the school time table needs working out, and so on. You could gain a lot of real experience of applied computer uses this way.

*Practical work experience.* Social studies courses in years 10 and 11 often contain an element of 'work experience' which it is wise not to ignore. Your careers or other teacher makes arrangements for you to spend a period of time, perhaps a week or two, with a local employer as if you were an ordinary employee – that is, you go to work in the morning, sign on if necessary, and are treated exactly like other employees. Usually the school makes sure that you are protected from exploitation – in the sense of being made to do unsuitable or repetitive work.

The idea is not so much to help you find out whether that particular business or line of work would interest you, but more to show some of the factors that being at work, or 'having a job', involves. You must get up on time and plan your journey to arrive on time. You must plan and execute work throughout the day, without the regular breaks provided by the school time table. You must manage money for fares and meals (although you are not paid a wage or salary for this 'job'). You have to learn to deal with other people, not necessarily of your own age or background.

At the end of the period, you may or may not have decided that you would like to go in for the kind of work you have experienced – perhaps engineering or hairdressing – but at least you will have understood something of what going to work is actually like.

*Experience from courses.* In addition to the general careers and work experience described above, you may gain experience from following certain courses. For example, you might be taking a social studies or child development course with some practical work in a local centre for old people or a nursery school. Young people are often a great help to nursery teachers with many three to five year olds to keep stimulated and happy each day. They can, for example, take over the supervision of play with sand and water – which isn't just play, but a way for very small children to learn about measuring, touching and feeling, and how to behave with other people. They are also able to listen to small children who are learning to read, help with their elementary efforts at maths, take them to local libraries with their teacher and generally learn about both how nursery and primary schools are run, and how young children grow and learn.

This sort of experience is helpful for anyone who might eventually become a parent, but it will be of especial use for those wishing to lay the foundations for a career in the 'caring' or 'helping' professions (in the Health Service, or social services, for example) or in teaching.

# Voluntary work

Finally, while still at school, you may gain work experience, fill in time, or even have fun with a host of voluntary activities. These will help you to find out about what you especially like doing and will also show future college recruiters or potential employers what sort of person you are.

In most neighbourhoods there are organisations that aim to look after the welfare of old people, for example. They are frequently glad to find young people who are prepared to give a little of their time on a regular basis to help (or even just to chat to) elderly people. For instance, an old person living alone some-times needs things done around the house which are simple for a strong, able-bodied person – like moving furniture, packing things away, cleaning the windows, or digging the garden – and this is where you could help.

Youth clubs also often use young people as junior leaders or assistants. So, if a camping or canoeing trip is being organised you can help with that, or you may be asked to invite speakers, or to arrange happenings such as discos or parties.

Most charities or campaigning organisations have offices requiring sensible volunteers. Sometimes newsletters need pro-ducing and circulating, membership lists need updating, and filing and other clerical tasks need to be brought up-to-date. Many groups depend on people who will give their time free of charge to assist in these and other ways; if you do, you may learn a great deal about the administration and running of organisa-tions, which will stand you in good stead in numerous other settings later.

Amateur theatrical groups, swimming clubs, anglers' associa-tions, Save-The-Whale campaigners, even the youth branches of political parties, all need help in circularising members, arran-ging productions, competitions and so forth. By volunteering to help, as well as to participate, you can learn a good deal about, for example, how your local neighbourhood operates, how compe-titive sport is run or how to attract audiences to performances! All this can be of use in the future.

# Chapter 3

# Choices at 16

When you are 16, you are legally entitled to leave school and there are some jobs you can do at this stage. Some of them will depend on your being fit and strong, some will be quite routine, even dead-end and boring, some may have training prospects built into them; but only a very few will be high-earning.

For some young people the immediate freedom and independence which leaving school and earning money of their own seem to bring, outweigh in attraction the extra qualifications which may be gained by staying on in full-time education. For others, whose families may be in severe economic circumstances, the prospect of extra income, whether from earnings or from state benefits, makes remaining in full-time education hard to contemplate.

However, unless you already have a successful rock band, or a dad who wants you to start at the bottom of the family firm, you would be well advised to think very carefully before simply deciding to leave school at the first opportunity – however attractive that may seem!

The main possibilities before you now are: to stay on in full-time education; to look for work with training built in; to look for any kind of work; to join a Youth Training scheme and hope that work will be forthcoming at the end of it; to register as unemployed and consider how best to find employment; or, even, to register as unemployed and give up all hope! Let's try to avoid the last possibility by looking at the other ones.

# More qualifications: full-time education

If at all possible, staying in full-time education is by far the best choice you can make. Better pay and prospects (not to mention a more satisfying quality of life) come more easily to those who have both more education – in the widest sense – and more qualifications. And, although it is also possible to study part time in several different ways, it is much harder to turn your mind to learning, particularly if you want exam qualifications, after a day's work.

What is more, if you stay on at school for a year or even two, you can rectify mistakes that may have led you into courses for which you were not suited in years 10 and 11; pick up passes in exams you previously failed, and add to your exam results; start on quite new types of courses not previously open to you; prepare for A levels, GNVQs or other advanced qualifications; consider the prospects of higher education; and take more time to find out precisely what sort of work would really suit you in the future.

Foundation courses are offered which prepare you for a range of possible jobs – office studies, catering, printing, engineering, social services and many more. If you take and succeed in one of these courses, you can start higher up a career ladder, with more interest, responsibility and pay than if you enter straight from school. A course often makes you think again, as well, about what you like or don't like, and what you are good at or not. It can also widen your ideas and choices: you'll find out about jobs you've never heard of, and through placements undertaken during the course, as well as contacts of the staff with employers, you may get introductions which would not otherwise be open to you.

You can also start doing a lot of new things for fun, as even the most traditionally run schools usually feel that students aged 16 and over deserve some sort of separate treatment. If you go to a sixth form, sixth form college or further education college, you will be treated differently from school. You will be encouraged to develop different ways of working, aimed at making you become more independent of both teachers and other classmates as you follow your own interests.

## GNVQs

GNVQs (General National Vocational Qualifications) are alternatives to GCE A levels or more GCSEs. They are normally taken by those who are still in full-time education, and can be taken alongside GCSEs or A levels, but are also available through part-time courses. They offer qualifications for work in areas such as business, manufacturing, information technology and health and social care. GNVQs are gained unit by unit, and are assessed by both coursework and external exams. The Foundation GNVQs are equivalent to four GCSEs at grades D–G, and Intermediate GNVQs are equivalent to four or five GCSEs at grades A–C. Both normally take one year of full-time study and can lead straight into a job, or into study for the next GNVQ level. Advanced GNVQs, which are designed as 'vocational A levels' are equivalent to two GCE A levels and normally take two years of full-time study, and can lead to higher education as well as into a job.

Subjects for GNVQs include art and design, business, construction and the built environment, engineering, health and social care, hospitality and catering, information technology, leisure and tourism, manufacturing, media, retail and distributive services, management studies, and science. From September 1997 land and environment, and performing arts and entertainment industries will be available. GNVQs can lead to more specialised NVQs (see page 28).

In Scotland the equivalent qualifications are GSVQs (General Scottish Vocational Qualifications) at Levels I, II and III. They are made up of individual units or modules, some of which may be optional rather than compulsory.

## Other courses

Apart from courses which can lead you directly on to higher education, there are many full-time courses on offer locally at schools and further education centres which improve your general education, and prepare you vocationally. You can take foundation and pre-entry courses of all sorts and the best way of finding out what possibilities there are is to obtain a copy of the booklet or prospectus that colleges always publish. You will find it in the local library, or simply by asking the college direct. Drop in and visit if you have questions. Remember, the colleges have to pay their way too, and the more students they attract the happier they are! They want to be of help, and have skilled staff available to advise you on what they offer and how you might fit into it.

# Part-time study

Even after you start your first job, you can gain extra qualifications through part-time college courses financed by your employer, courses at local adult education colleges, work-assessed NVQs (see below) and distance learning (studying at home) which can lead to membership of a professional institute, such as the Chartered Association of Certified Accountants.

You will have gathered already that all sorts of arrangements are made by colleges and employers to allow you to study part time if you cannot or do not want to stay in full-time education after your sixteenth birthday. Obviously, if you get a job at 16 nobody is going to force you to study against your will; all you have to do is to accept a job which has no in-service training built into it. But it is widely recognised that most young people are quite capable of holding a job, of studying to improve the way they do it and of learning to do more complex work as time goes on.

The advantage to employers of releasing young people for on-the-job training is clear. They can choose the type of young person they want and then make sure that he or she is trained to develop skills they will need in their future workplace. The expense of having staff on training programmes is repaid by having staff qualified and experienced in exactly the ways required. Some of this on-the-job training is related to the specific needs of a particular employer, sometimes to a particular trade or industry. If you undertake part-time, job-related training, you may be preparing yourself for a career with that particular employer, or for promotion and development in the industry, but with different employers. Some firms specify the period they expect you to continue in their employment on completion of studies or training, while others make no conditions.

Study related to your employment varies from one or several short full-time courses, through release for varying periods, to full-time secondment. You can go to the company or industry training centre specially equipped and aimed at your particular type of job, or you can follow courses with students from a variety of backgrounds at local colleges, combining study with practical experience. You will usually be aiming at particular qualifications, which may be general awards of GCSE and A level, Intermediate or Advanced GNVQ, a BTEC or City and Guilds (see below); or professional qualifications relevant to the industry you are in, such as accountancy, banking or engineering; or they may be formal degree courses.

Phrases used in this connection are curiously self-explanatory. 'Day-release' means you combine work and study by taking one day a week for a given period of time to go to a local college for specific, job-related course work. 'Block-release' means that you are released from the workplace for a specified period of full-time study in a 'block' of time, instead of one day at a time. A 'sandwich' course involves extensive periods of both practical and academic work; you will study for a prolonged period, return to work and again go back to the place of study for completion. 'Secondment' involves the release of the employee for a full-time course of study which may vary in length, often leading to post-experience qualifications (at either basic or more advanced levels) which are offered in further or higher education centres.

# Further qualifications

## NVQs (National Vocational Qualifications)

NVQs have to be assessed on work done at the workplace, though they are also awarded at colleges, through work experience done during the course. The great thing about them is that there are no set time limits for when they are achieved, so each person is assessed on their competence in a particular activity when ready, and eventually a certificate is issued when enough 'units of competence' have been gained.

NVQs are designed to go from Level 1 up to Level 5, equivalent to a top professional qualification; with Level 3 roughly equivalent to an A level. They can be added to at any point in a person's working life, to give employers throughout the UK (in Scotland they are known as SVQs), and eventually across Europe, a clear idea of what a candidate for a job is capable of doing.

The assessments are carried out in offices and factories and other workplaces by the employers, and the assessments are approved and the certificates awarded by 'lead bodies' such as City and Guilds, RSA, BTEC and the organisations that head different industries, such as construction, catering and journalism. Other areas of work in which you can gain NVQs include retailing, travel services, hospitality, health and social care, child care and financial services.

## Royal Society of Arts examinations

RSA examinations are mainly qualifications for office and commercial work – secretarial and clerical. They can be taken at school, contributing to GCSEs and GNVQs; RSA/GCSE subjects are keyboarding applications, information technology, economics and statistics. RSA examinations are normally taken by people studying through further or adult education, who may already be in a job, which means they can also count towards NVQ qualifications up to Level 3.

The types of qualification available from RSA include GCSEs, GNVQs and NVQs, as well as the RSA's own examinations. The GCSEs include business studies, design and technology, information studies and information systems. The GNVQs are available in all subject areas and levels. The NVQs cover a wide range of occupational areas including administration, marketing, management, journalism, sport and recreation and transport. RSA's own examinations are available at three stages and include text processing examinations as well as other business-related subjects. They are mainly for students in schools, colleges and adult education centres who are doing clerical, secretarial and business courses.

As office technology develops, RSA examinations keep up with the new skills needed; subjects range from basic typing, audio typing and shorthand to word processing, desktop publishing, keyboarding applications, and typing or word-processing in French and German. Modern language examinations include languages for commercial purposes. Companies that do a lot of exporting or have branches overseas would find these very attractive qualifications.

## London Chamber of Commerce and Industry (LCCI)

Like the RSA examinations, those of the LCCI are business related and are for people working in offices. They cover subjects such as shorthand, typing, word-processing, bookkeeping and accounts, information processing, and languages for industry and commerce, plus marketing, purchasing, public relations and 'euroqualifications' (a European Executive Assistant Certificate, a Diploma in European Business Administration, and a Commercial Language Assistant Certificate).

## City and Guilds

City and Guilds (C&G) qualifications cover all kinds of subjects, many of which are craft-based: plumbing, beauty therapy, oxy-acetylene welding, bakery, animal care, travel studies and vehicle restoration, as well as many more. They are closely linked with NVQs and are awarded at several levels, up to FCGI (Fellowship), in recognition of technical excellence, rather than purely academic achievement.

Courses are offered at colleges of further education, training centres, training companies and adult education institutes. There are full-time courses in community care, catering and hairdressing; other courses are part time.

## BTEC and SCOTVEC

These courses are also offered either through part-time college study, or full time. The certificates and diplomas are offered at three levels: First, National and Higher National; a BTEC National is roughly equivalent to A levels and takes two years full time or three years part time. An HNC or HND (Higher National Certificate or Diploma) is roughly equivalent to a degree; the certificate course is usually taken part time, while the diploma course is full time and covers a broader range of subjects. There are no entry requirements for First certificate and diploma courses, but for National and Higher National courses entry qualifications are needed.

SCOTVEC courses are made up of different units or modules, for both full-time and part-time students and trainees. Colleges offer different modular programmes, which can include any number and any combination of modules, some optional, and some compulsory. It is best to get in touch with colleges to find out what they offer. After an HND you may be able to go straight into the second or third year of a degree course. In Scotland there is also the RET: Record of Education and Training, which is a computer-based record of any new SCOTVEC or SVQ module, unit or course qualifications that are gained throughout a person's career.

# Training for young people

For those who do not want to stay on at school, or go into further education, a programme of youth training or a Modern

Apprenticeship can lead directly into a job. Programmes offer training in a variety of jobs, such as hairdressing, agriculture, engineering, catering, construction and various other industries. They are run by employers, colleges, training companies, local authorities and some voluntary organisations and approved by local TECs (Training and Enterprise Councils).

A training plan gives the opportunity to gain NVQs and other qualifications through off-the-job training at a college, training centre or employer's training school, with the chance to use computers and information technology, if appropriate.

During training you are paid a training allowance of £29.50 if aged 16, and at least £35 per week if aged 17 or over; you may also qualify for extra help with travel and lodging costs. Your employer may also give you a top-up wage. Even if you already have a job, you may find that your employer puts you on to a training programme for the training you need. The local TEC or careers offices are the places to go to if you want information about local training programmes.

When you are thinking about which jobs to choose (see next chapter), the opportunity for training is one of the aspects you need to take into account.

## Modern Apprenticeships

A Modern Apprenticeship, which is for 16 and 17 year olds, combines employment and training. Around 40 different industries have developed their own Modern Apprenticeships, with qualifications leading to jobs at technician, craft and junior management level that are recognised throughout the industry. These include child care and the travel industry. The apprenticeship takes about three years and offers training up to at least NVQ level 3, which is similar to two A levels or an Advanced GNVQ. Ninety per cent of those doing a modern apprenticeship are employed and receive a salary; those who are not fully employed usually have their training allowance topped up by the employer. Full details of Modern Apprenticeships are available from jobcentres and local TECs as well as the careers services.

# Youth Credits

If you leave school or college at 16 or 17 and already have a job or are looking for a job, you can use Youth Credits to buy training. The value of the credits can range from £750 to over £5000, depending on what you need, and on the type of industry you are in. The type of training a Youth Credit can buy is a Modern Apprenticeship, or work-based training through a TEC; both will lead to NVQs.

Youth Credits may have different names in different parts of the country, such as Career Link or Training Credits, and can take different forms – you may be given a cheque book, a plastic card, or a passport which you use to buy the same value of training. They give you a planned programme of training for work plus a paid wage or a training allowance. The training is usually given at work, often with a part-time college course. Information on Youth Credits is available from jobcentres and TECs.

# Chapter 4

# Selecting Jobs

Now, just as you did when you thought about what subjects to take at GCSE and A level, you need to think about yourself and your interests, your talents and experiences, in deciding on the work you'd like to try.

## Workplaces

Think of work settings: can you bear to be indoors all day? Would you prefer to be out and about? Agriculture, construction, the armed services, selling – all offer outdoor work at many levels. Alternatively, you may prefer an indoor life, but not in an office – factories of all sorts, hospitals, schools, libraries, laboratories, television or recording studios are some examples of places where you could work.

Offices are interesting workplaces, with every business of whatever sort needing them. Various skills are required: can you handle enquiries by callers or on the telephone? Do you like sorting and filing information, organising meetings, drafting reports or minutes, persuading people, keeping books or stock records, making things run smoothly? If so, office work may interest you.

Perhaps you like seeing new people all the time and don't mind chatting to strangers – reception and interviewing work ranges from doing market and opinion research for products and services, through making travel arrangements, to arranging housing allocations for people in need, or sorting out who is entitled to a rate rebate or to extra supplementary benefits.

Certain courses not only equip you with information relevant to some of these areas of work, but also help you develop the skills you require to deal with people in your job. Think of it this way, in a context familiar to you: your school maths teacher was prepared for his or her work by learning all about maths, but also by being taught how to pass all that knowledge on to you, to bring out your capacities, and to plan courses for you to follow – in other words a teacher must be taught how to teach, as well as what to teach – and that applies to many lines of work.

# Classifying work by type of industry

Another way you can look at jobs is to think of them as relating to one of three types of industry: primary (or basic); manufacturing; and service industries.

In the first type, jobs have to do with extracting the *basic* raw materials we need in society out of the earth and sea, for instance, in mining, in forestry and agriculture, or fishing.

*Manufacturing* covers those jobs which take raw materials and make goods and products from them, or which make other products from those first manufactured. So, oil gives range to a plethora of oil-based materials – plastics, for example – and these are used to make other things, such as fabrics, utensils, or equipment. Fish is first caught, then it is frozen, or made into fish fingers, or fish meal for animal food.

The *service* industries cover those jobs dealing with people, in the broadest possible way. The education services require teachers, careers officers, canteen staff and catering organisers; the retail services, people working in stores and shops; the social services, social workers and others caring for the vulnerable; the administrative services, office workers; the transport services, pilots and bus drivers and many others; the financial services, bank clerks and accountants; the catering services, meals-on-wheels organisers as well as café proprietors, and so on.

If you would like to work near where you spent your schooldays, you would be wise to find out which industries employ most people locally, and what training or qualification, if any, they require. You will often find that, where particular industries dominate the locality, colleges offer special courses relating to those industries which are not available in other parts of the country.

Remember that the technological revolution didn't stop when Stevenson designed the Rocket. So-called unskilled or semiskilled jobs are disappearing fast as machinery is developed which can make them redundant. More and more technical skills are required from all of us, and these mean a better basic education and qualifications. Nowadays, you need to be versatile; you must be able to master more than one skill, and to do more than carry out simple repetitive operations. So, the more qualifications you have when you start, the more likely you are to start in a job at a higher level, and to turn that job into a satisfying career.

# Things, data or people?

Another way of considering the world of work is to put aside the idea of different classifications of industry, and to see whether the jobs involve work with things, data or people.

## Things

This predominantly involves working with tools, machinery, vehicles, and other mechanical or electrical equipment. Obviously people and data will come into it, but the main focus of your work will be with equipment and machinery. This in itself varies from using separate tools for specific work – domestic plumbing say, or jewellery-making – to operating machinery: sometimes supervising the same function being carried out again and again, sometimes seeing through a complete, multiple process. Using transport machinery is different again and demands different skills and qualities from the worker; and jobs requiring the use of equipment for testing, exploring, surveying or researching could almost be said to belong to categories of work involving data.

## Data

This sort of work used to be called paperwork, but the new technologies mean that, today, much data – information, facts, figures, statistics – is stored, analysed and spread about by computers, word-processors, fax machines and other electronic devices, rather than in files, letters and ledgers. Certainly things and people are also involved, but the main part of the work is concerned with reading, communicating, analysing, recording, calculating and solving problems with the use of knowledge.

## People

Working with people doesn't necessarily eliminate working with things or data, of course, but the point of this particular employment is the people for whom and with whom it is done. For instance, nurses and teachers note data – how high the temperature is, how many passed the maths test – and use things – thermometers, bedpans, kidney machines, blackboards, calculators and tape recorders – but the patients and students are the focus of their work. Working with people, whether you are a waitress or a clerk in the post office, involves as a main task being able to listen and talk, understand how others feel, maybe persuade and even direct them, settle disputes and offer advice.

# What do you like doing?

Your interests outside school subjects tell something about your potential skills, personal qualities and aptitudes. For instance, here is a list of things people often like to do, outside school time:

- Babysitting, going on sponsored walks. Already you're showing you are interested in helping people with problems and many jobs do just that – nurses, people in all branches of social services, occupational therapists and police, for example.
- Model-making, fixing things, woodwork and metalwork, cars and motor bikes. These practical interests may lead to work in

various kinds of engineering, building, plumbing or welding, for instance.

- Running clubs, organising discos, fund-raising. Such experience is useful in a variety of jobs to do with other people, with persuading, influencing and organising them – perhaps in the travel business, in personnel management, in banks and shops and post offices.

There are many more activities you undertake – reading, perhaps, or acting – which can give you ideas about future jobs. And, of course, as we've noted before, your school and especially your examination subjects will narrow down the field for you.

# What are you good at?

Apart from your interests, what do you think you are good at? There's no point being coy and saying 'oo-er nothing much' unless you really want nothing much by way of work later.

Being good at things is not just a case of having top marks in the maths test, or being able to draw a portrait that really looks like someone, though these talents are a help. Are you quick at fitting things together as in jigsaw puzzles? This will be helpful in sorting and craft work. Are you neat and fast at preparing and storing things – your kit for games, your breakfast, your homework? Many office jobs, for example, depend on fast execution and tidy record-keeping. Are you good at finding things out – looking up references, asking people questions that get full answers? Information-gathering work of all sorts (in journalism, publishing and market research, etc) needs that quality.

You may find, for instance, that *selling* is really exciting – perhaps you have run a stall at a school jumble sale. It doesn't much matter, at first, what you sell; you just enjoy shifting something on to someone else. Many captains of industry first started by selling, and it is, of course, at the base of all business activities. The capacity to sell may lead you from a stall in a street market to the board of Marks & Spencer – but don't forget that it's not only people with shops who sell things. Large construction companies have to persuade people to buy their bridges, or motorways; fruit farmers have to persuade people to buy pears or strawberries; film-makers have to persuade people to watch their movies.

Selling, then, is just one example of a skill or aptitude you may have, which can be used across a range of products. However, business requires many other talents: money management, advertising, product research, forward planning and administration. Courses in business studies and economics can prepare you well for a management career across a whole range of fields and professional courses in accountancy may open many avenues in private as well as public organisations. Science-based courses may equally well lead you to private commerce – developing new household products, foodstuffs, or pharmaceutical drugs, for instance – or to research into space travel, or work in hospital laboratories such as testing blood samples, developing X-rays or analysing brain-scans.

## School subjects

Knowing what subjects you are good at, and what jobs they lead to, may help you. If maths and sciences come easily to you, careers in banking, computers, construction, statistics, bookkeeping and surveying jump to mind. In a more specifically scientific side you could move into the medical world, pharmaceuticals, dietetics, horticulture, nuclear physics, engineering or mining.

Good English is essential to almost everything, but if language is your special flair, then marketing, secretarial work, librarianship, broadcasting and publishing are possibilities. Foreign languages can take you into the hotel and tourism business, translation and interpreting or the travel industry.

Geography can lead to travel, town planning, surveying and geology, while history is useful to archaeology, work in galleries and museums, law or local government.

Art and design interests can take you into advertising, illustration, photography, all kinds of designing, and so on.

If the more academic subjects are not your main strength, think of things you do like. If you are good at swimming you can take coaching qualifications and find employment at baths, leisure centres, or in schools. If you really like teaching sport, it may motivate you enough to study other subjects, so that you can get a BEd degree or PGCE (Postgraduate Certificate of Education) specialising in physical education, and get a job as a PE teacher. On the other hand, there is a growing amount of work in the leisure industries generally – for instance, in sports centres and private sports clubs, climbing and skiing resorts, water sports and boating, developing and selling special kit and equipment.

Sometimes you can't think what you're good at, but your friends can – and you can always point out what other people you know do well or badly. If you find it difficult to think about yourself, ask someone who knows you well to help.

## What are your weak points?

The opposite of knowing what you are good at means recognising where you are weak. If you know where you are less strong, you can either avoid thinking about certain types of work where your weak points would matter or, if possible, you can set about improving yourself. There's no point, for instance, in setting your heart on being an airline pilot if you are terribly short-sighted, or on being a commercial artist if you are colour blind! If chemistry is not your strong point, you'll probably reject pharmacy as a career; on the other hand, you could make a big effort to improve if, for instance, you really want to be a beautician.

## Are you fit?

Think, too, about your personal health – physical fitness is not in itself vital to most jobs – though obviously labourers, professional sportsmen and women, physical education teachers, divers and airline pilots among many others, need to be in tiptop condition – but it is important to be in good health for work generally. If you often have to take time off, it is inconvenient for colleagues who must cover for you, it means work gets behind and your own reputation for reliability suffers. On the other hand, some kinds of work are positively harmful to your health unless both you and your employer take good precautions – sitting for long hours on unsuitable chairs may give you back and hip problems, repetitive movements on a fast word-processor can give you RSI (Repetitive Strain Injury), dirty heavy work needs special amenities, machinery needs safety guards, and buildings must be carefully designed and maintained for work purposes.

# Your attitudes towards work

Your personality and character show in all sorts of ways. People who like to do things on their own will find quite different work appealing to them compared with those who like to be with others constantly. For some, the atmosphere at work is more important than what they actually do; some prefer to deal with problems without worrying about time, others prefer to work at a steady pace and stop and start at regular times; others, finally, don't mind working in shifts, taking time off when most folk are at work.

Some people are concerned about whether their work is interesting and generally useful and whether it offers them a challenge; for others, the most important thing is the pay, irrespective of the prospects or of anything else. You must try to sort out for yourself what your own attitude is so that you know both what you are offering to a prospective employer, and what is being offered to you.

It is important to remember, for instance, that at school most of your work was done by you alone; *you* were the one whose work was being marked, writing a project, painting a picture, or playing an instrument (although some of this may have been done with others, for example when playing in a band or orchestra or making a mural or display with a group). Almost *all* sorts of work, however, involve a close relationship between co-workers or colleagues. In addition to your own energies and initiatives, employers will expect you to get on with other people quite easily and to be alert to their needs and feelings, as well as your own. If you can find ways of showing that you are interested in the actual business of the firm or service to which you are applying yourself, that too will help. For, although many kinds of work are the same whatever the setting, the quality of the end product is always important. Your boss will want to know not only that you are neat and careful with the order books, but also that you have some regard for what is being ordered and don't actively hate it!

# What do you want from a job?

You will put into your job some of the most important facets of yourself: your time, effort, skills, training, aspirations and ambitions. You have a responsibility to yourself to ensure that you will get adequate compensation for this input. There are a great many rewards that a job may offer. The following may help in developing a comprehensive list of what you need and want.

## Opportunity for developing your skills

You may have training, for instance in computer studies, that has provided you with some raw skills which can only be developed to a practical and productive level through actual work experience. Indeed, without a real-life application of your training, it will probably have been a waste of time. More positively, an appropriate job will give you the opportunity for developing your earlier training. Your education or training has provided you with a general level of competence which can act as a foundation to learning new skills offered to you at work. These skills may be specific, such as learning a computer application, or general, such as learning about communication in organisations. Both types will be useful in your career development.

## General work experience

You may not be sure as to where you are going or precisely what you want. Maybe your future will become clearer with the experience and maturity that you will get from a responsible job in the 'real' world. Your first job can provide this general work experience.

## Opportunity for self-improvement

You may be seeking development in some specific areas and believe that this will best be gained in a demanding work environment. For example, a job may provide an opportunity for improving social skills, confidence, poise, or communication with people in authority.

If self-development or career ambitions are not high on your agenda, making new friends and acquaintances may be of equal or higher importance.

## Money

You may want a job which will provide you with substantial income because this will bring you the freedom, independence and material things that you are after. Jobs with relatively high salaries may be available but they could be short on providing for your other needs.

In these uncertain times, you may fear committing yourself to an organisation which cannot guarantee long-term employment. Secure employment is particularly important if you have regular loan repayments on, say, a car.

## Social standing

Many jobs and organisations offer a certain status to the new employee because of the respect that these jobs hold in the community. The prestige offered by such an association can be very compelling, for instance a graduate accountant may strongly prefer working with one of the larger international firms rather than a local office.

## Challenge

The opportunity of proving yourself in a complex, new and competitive environment may be the aspect of a job which most attracts you.

Or perhaps the prospect of a position of power, authority, leadership or control appeals to you. Most new employees are not placed in such situations early in their careers but some jobs can offer this in a reasonably short time, such as officer training in the armed services.

## Pros and cons

It is likely that you will seek many of the above qualities in your first job, and many of them may overlap in any particular job. List, in order of preference, those aspects of a potential job that you would prefer it to have, indicating those which are essential and then those which are important. You should also list those aspects that you find unattractive. Some job seekers avoid multinationals; producers or sellers of unethical products; jobs which involve selling; jobs which require extensive travel.

Attach a list of negative attributes to your list of positive ones, indicating those that are totally unacceptable and those you strongly dislike. The combined lists can be used in evaluating alternatives.

The next step is to check your lists and the order in which you have placed the various job attributes. To do this, picture yourself how you would like to be in five years' and 20 years' time. Are your present lists of wants and dislikes in a potential job consistent with these pictures? Now reconsider each entry. Is it more important or less important in the perspective of your ambitions? Adjust your priorities where you think it is necessary.

# What do you bring to the job?

You have thought about what you want from a job. Now you

need to consider those attributes of yourself, good and bad, that you will bring to, and probably use in, your new job.

There are two objectives in carrying out this self-assessment. Obviously, knowing yourself better will both help you in selecting a suitable job and assembling wide-ranging information on yourself that you will need for job applications and interviews.

## Motivation

In looking at what you want from a job you have been indirectly saying something about what it is that drives, excites and motivates you.

There are five areas in which we all, to a lesser or greater degree, have needs for fulfilment. Understanding each area and its significance in your psychological make-up helps you to gain a knowledge of yourself and therefore what sort of job will best suit you:

*Security.* A mortgage-free home; a happy marriage with children; a stable and permanent job; lack of money worries; a clear conscience; and a well-balanced and happy disposition are all aspects of the need that most people have for a safe and secure existence.

*Social relationships.* People have a need to be part of groups. We like to have social contact and close relationships within the family. We enjoy having networks of friends and acquaintances and like to participate in activities with others and to develop warm friendships. We are social animals and have strong needs for a wide range of social relationships.

*Success.* Many people have a strong desire to be a success. This could include achieving a position of prominence in society, being successful in a career or profession, owning enviable material possessions, and being looked up to by fellow workers, friends and family.

*Dominance.* Some people have a need to be in positions of

authority or power. They may wish to be leaders and exert influence and control over others.

*Task satisfaction.* People who carry out their tasks well, are constantly striving to do things better and to do work of the highest quality, are those who are proud of doing a good job. Such people get enjoyment out of the actual activity of work. This motivation often extends into the general areas of their life and they may have many interests and pursuits that provide opportunity for self-development.

Which of the five basic needs discussed above dominate your make-up? Most people have all of them present but you can often find that one or two seem to be more important. Put your thoughts into a pie chart which shows the relative importance of each of them to you. It may be an interesting model for understanding yourself and others and it can be used in deciding between different job alternatives.

Make sure that you date your chart. The relative strengths of your

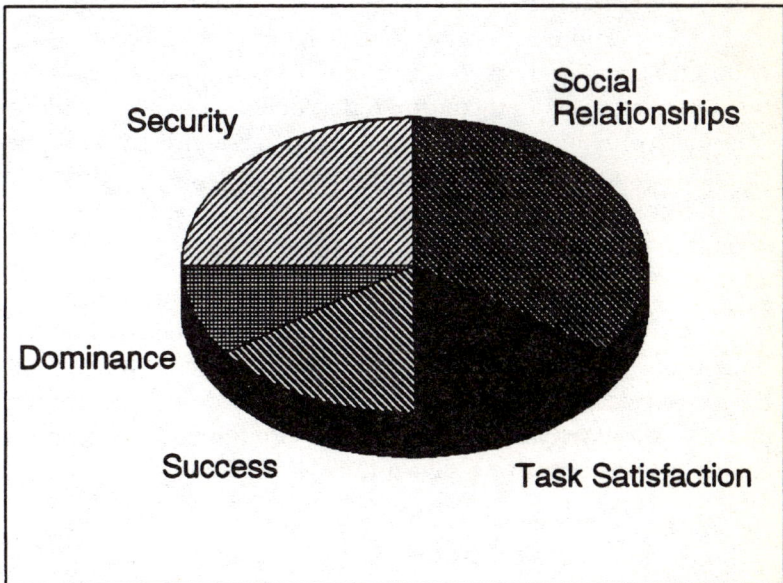

**Figure 1** *Relative importance of my motivations*

different motivations will vary as your experience and circumstances change. It may provide an interesting insight into the way in which you view the world today when, in the future, you look back and compare it with an updated chart.

## Strengths and weaknesses

Another way of learning about yourself is to investigate your strengths and weaknesses in areas relevant to your intended work experience. This may all seem obvious and trite. Of course, if you are going to choose a job suited to you it must provide scope for your strong points and you must not rely, for your success in the job, on performance in areas in which you are weak. Also, when you apply for a job, you will need to emphasise your good points and play down the poor ones. It is clear that there is a need to know what they are. But do you?

It is so important for you to identify and come to terms with all your major attributes and failings that you need to go through a thorough and disciplined process, even though it may be laborious and seem unnecessary. Most people believe that they have a fairly good appreciation of their strengths and weaknesses without a lot of analysis. It is not until they go through the process of trying to write them down that they realise how shallow was their previous understanding. You have already thought about your skills and aptitudes in school-related subjects, work experience and physical ability. Now you can evaluate your strengths and weaknesses in the following areas.

*Personality.* List at least five aspects of your personality which will help you in the work environment and five which would be unhelpful. You may find this difficult. Do not be put off or become frustrated. Persevere. Put your list aside for a few days and revise it. It may be necessary to go through this procedure a couple of times until you have a fully descriptive list.

*Appearance.* How well or poorly do you impress people? Are you well-groomed, physically attractive, pleasant and friendly? Do you make a strong initial impression? Do you have any weak aspects in your image?

*Training.* Relevant training is obviously a strength when considering how well suited you might be for a particular job. But seemingly unrelated education or training could indicate an aptitude for some aspect of a potential job. So, on your list of strengths put down all the courses that you have done, particularly those in which you have done well.

*Personal relationships.* Effectiveness in many jobs depends upon interpersonal skills. Do you have any strengths or weaknesses in communicating with others, in influencing them, in understanding their situations or in getting them to like you? Can you work easily with others; do you fit in quickly; do you gain acceptance from groups; do you put people at ease? Skills or

**Table 1**  *My strengths and weaknesses*

|  | **Strengths** | **Weaknesses** |
|---|---|---|
| **Skills** | numerical<br>problem solving<br>musical appreciation | vocabulary<br>writing ability |
| **Personality** | gregarious<br>well liked<br>sense of humour<br>hard-working<br>honest | easily offended<br>hold grudges |
| **Physical ability** | overall fitness | poor eyesight<br>smoke |
| **Appearance** | smart dresser<br>slim | |
| **Training** | good formal school<br>training | no training outside<br>school |
| **Work experience** | | none |
| **Personal relationships** | work very well in a<br>team environment | |
| **Social status** | private school<br>background | |

deficiencies in these areas are important to job enjoyment and success and, therefore, to the selection process.

*Social status.* As much as we may like to think it is not so, your social background may be a strength or weakness for some particular job. Your class, religion, school, sex, even your address may have an effect on your job application, positive or negative. You may find discrimination unacceptable, but recognise that it does exist and may be applied to you.

You now have a list of your strengths and weaknesses which might apply to a potential work situation. Obviously, there is more to you than this. The list does not include the myriad aspects to yourself which are neutral or non-job related. Nevertheless, it will be a helpful tool in deciding between job alternatives, as you will see later.

Preparing such a list is a highly subjective undertaking. It is quite common and natural for many people in preparing it to exaggerate favourable points and minimise or neglect unpleasant ones. Similarly, many go the other way and understate qualities and over-emphasise weaknesses. Therefore, it is a good idea to get feedback from someone who knows you well and with whom you are comfortable in disclosing an intimate picture of yourself. Hopefully, this will help you to develop an accurate and well-balanced list.

## Interests

Apart from attributes directly relevant to your potential job, you will take to that new job many interests which may tell you and a prospective employer something about whether a particular job is suited to you.

*Hobbies.* What you choose to do in your own time can tell a great deal about which jobs may be suited to you. For instance, model plane building may indicate perseverance or attention to detail. On the other hand, it may indicate reluctance for social contact. The interpretation should not be left entirely to the potential employer, who will tend to estimate the relevance of your hobbies from his own set of values and prejudices. If you have a hobby which takes up a lot of your time and will attract attention, you should put forward your own views as to its qualities relevant to the job.

*Sporting interests.* Many organisations have a culture of shared sporting interests. Because the interest is external and not related to work performance, it can be a powerful force uniting different levels of an organisation and promoting internal communication. A potential employer may see an interest that an applicant may have in what is also the firm's sport as evidence that he or she will be more readily accepted in the work environment. This may be enough to tip the balance between two comparable candidates.

Playing a sport, particularly if it is competitive or a team sport, may be highly attractive. Positive discrimination for sport is entrenched in many firms. This often has as much to do with the egos of the executives who control them and hence achieve some kudos by association or ownership, as it does to any marketing benefit it may offer the organisation.

For most organisations operating in our sports-orientated society, all sorts of positive job attributes will be attached to people who are successful in sport, especially in a leadership capacity.

*Self-development.* Many people have strong interests in self-development. This can be expressed in diverse ways, for example:

- part-time or further education;
- reading for improvement;
- public speaking.

An interest in developing oneself can be so powerful that it can evolve into a 'motivator'. Those who are keen on self-development will not be satisfied for long with a job which does not allow for this need or, worse, is antagonistic to it.

## Values and attitudes

Schools and colleges generally try to promote a consistent set of attitudes and values. The new job seeker may have been cocooned within this experience and it may be quite a surprise to find that other institutions and organisations have very divergent ways of looking at things.

This does not mean that their values may be so different they seem immoral. But the inexperienced, possibly idealistic, newcomer to the 'real' world may find them unattractive or distasteful at first.

Adjustments to one's attitudes and values will generally take place as one's perspective changes. This process of maturing will continue for many years and the variation in outlook that takes place can be very surprising in retrospect.

It is difficult to predict how someone will behave when experiencing the inevitable clash of values that a new job will bring. Perhaps you should list your strongly held beliefs, attitudes and values that you could not bear to compromise on and eliminate job alternatives where this could happen.

## Achievements

What you would consider as a personal achievement is something for which you have had to work hard and/or is something for which you have talent. An achievement tells a great deal about yourself. It may indicate an interest or motivation which could be of paramount importance in targeting your first job. People generally enjoy doing what they are good at. So list your accomplishments and see what the list tells you about yourself.

It is not important that your list of achievements be recognised as such by others. It is the significance to you which counts. Investigate your list and see if you can discover what it is that you really enjoy, and is important to you.

List your interests, values, attitudes and achievements. The table overleaf is an example of what you may have found about yourself. This list will be useful later when preparing CVs for different employers.

**Table 2**  *My interests, values, attitudes and achievements*

| Interests | collecting garden gnomes<br>reading science fiction stories<br>rugby league: spectator<br>squash: competition player<br>music |
| --- | --- |
| Values and attitudes | basic Christian ethics<br>dislike of discrimination<br>anti-war<br>anti-socialism |
| Achievements | captain of school sports team<br>top of class in English<br>Scouts/Guides medals<br>play guitar |

# Chapter 5

# The Jobs Market

One of the factors which will determine whether you do well in a job will be its environment and how you feel about it. We shall now look at some settings for work, bearing in mind that one of the main differences between employers is whether they are in what we call the public or the private sector.

## The public sector

Organisations in the public sector do business or offer services which do not have profit-making as their prime concern. Their main financing comes from grants or subsidies from various public systems of taxation – income tax, council tax, licence fees, etc. However, some aspects of the work are being subcontracted.

Local government, the NHS (National Health Service), the BBC, and the Civil Service (that is, government employees) are examples of major organisations of this type. In some areas, this sort of employer is the major source of work for the neighbourhood; for example, in local government.

The range of jobs offered here is enormous, and spreads from the mundane and routine, through to highly-paid professional and technical work.

## Local government

In *housing* alone, you can work in the building and decorating trades; as an estate manager; with homeless people; allocating properties; advising those who require accommodation; doing various forms of administration and finance (rents have to be collected and calculated); doing research into building techniques, housing needs, surveying and land use; or work as an architect.

The vast part of the *education* service is also run through local government – jobs exist for school and college teachers, for librarians and media resources officers, for planners and statisticians, for educational researchers, for canteen staff, school cleaners, secretaries, caretakers, groundsmen, laboratory technicians, architects, building workers, and administrators.

Many of the people who work in *caring* jobs are employed in local government social services departments – perhaps they look after elderly people in day centres or residential homes, or help in the homes of people who are too ill or infirm to look after themselves. Most nursery nurses are employed in local authority day nurseries and family centres for children under five. Caring for the mentally and physically handicapped provides many local authority jobs in day centres or residential homes.

Other local government work revolves around *money* – budgets have to be worked out each year for millions of pounds in many authorities, the community charge and rents have to be collected, grants negotiated with central government, loans organised and controlled for building programmes. Much work done for local authorities, for instance in rubbish collection and school catering, is now undertaken by private contract companies. So there is a good deal of work for bookkeepers and accountants, economists and planners, etc.

# National Health Service

The National Health Service is responsible for the majority of the hospitals in the country, for the local health centres, for some specialised work, often overlapping with local authority social services departments, with mental or physically ill or handicapped people, and for most doctors' practices.

In medicine itself, jobs range from those of surgeons and physicians, through technical and laboratory-based work, to all kinds of nursing. All sorts of paramedical jobs exist – for example in speech, physio and occupational therapy – for patients recovering from surgery or illness. The NHS also employs health visitors to go to people's homes and assess their needs there, as well as planners and researchers to advise on the management of people, equipment and money. Finally, porters and cleaners, cooks and administrators, receptionists and secretaries are all needed in hospitals, and some of them in health centres and doctors' surgeries.

# The private sector

This is the description given to enterprises whose prime intention is to make a profit (or at least not to make a loss) and who do not depend on public subsidies for long-term financial balance. Such enterprises cut across most types of commerce and industry and range from huge international corporations (like drugs and pharmaceuticals companies or car manufacturers) to businesses owned and operated by one person (perhaps a farrier or a solicitor). Much of the important work in all such enterprises involves the selling and promotion of the product or service offered in competition with others – a consideration less important, or even non-existent, in the public sector. For some people, the sense of competition and the need to sell is the most exciting part of the work, and private employers look for new recruits with a keen sense of how business ticks. A whole industry ancillary to selling has also grown up in the past decades to help people and firms with their public relations, advertising and promotion work.

# Working for a large organisation

Another major difference in work settings, evident in both public and private sectors, relates to the *size* of the organisation involved. There are advantages and disadvantages all round, of course, but let us look first at some of the pros and cons of working for a large organisation.

*Training and promotion.* Big corporations, public and private, often run their own in-service training and promotion schemes, so that once employed you can be sure that your skills and talents will be developed according to your capabilities and desires. You may be taken on at a junior level, and helped to rise steadily, with educational opportunities and promotion. This may mean moving about from one workplace to another, but can lead to a highly rewarding career development. Such employers pay for the fees and exam charges, give appropriate time off for study and pay higher salaries for greater qualifications.

*Security and pensions.* Many large operations, although they cannot always guarantee a job for life, make sure that suitable employees stay with them, absorbing them into changes and developments. For those who relish continuity, stability and security this may be a major advantage. Furthermore, most large companies have a superannuation, or pension, scheme which gives more benefit to those who have contributed to it longest. This will obviously be a welcome supplement to the state retirement pension when you arrive at the end of your working life.

*Fringe benefits.* Most big companies and public employers offer a variety of extra services and amenities which make working life more pleasant and sometimes better remunerated. Canteens with free or low-cost meals, good holiday and sickness schemes, season ticket loans, and help with house or car purchase are common. Recreation and sports facilities of a high standard are often made available by major employers, and social clubs of many kinds can help forge friendships among colleagues and workmates.

*Too large and impersonal.* The disadvantages of working in such large organisations are sometimes thought to include the comparative problems you may have of making your voice heard, or standing out from the crowd if you have a special contribution to make; the amount of administration to be gone through before anything can be done – 'Too much bureaucracy', you sometimes hear said – which may make it difficult to implement new ideas and get things done fast.

# Working for a small company

The advantages of working in a smaller operation are that your own initiative may be more quickly rewarded, you may have fewer people to work with and persuade to do things, and therefore feel more personally connected with both colleagues and the business in hand.

You need not necessarily miss out on the in-service training opportunities offered by larger employers, as many small operations take on trainees through 'training for young people', sending them to day-release college courses.

# Prospects

If we seem here to be concentrating on the importance of on-the-job training, it is because one of the major problems many young people encounter when they start work as early as 16 is that of boredom. As the youngest, newest employee you are frequently given the least interesting (and possibly the nastiest) work to do. This may be endured more easily if you know that the possibility exists of moving on to more interesting and better-paid work as time goes on. On the other hand, one of the most dispiriting aspects of your new work may be the knowledge that it will not change for the better.

Many young people try to deal with this by leaving the job and looking for another one. Until fairly recently they could quite easily drift in and out of one position after another without developing particular skills, so that at least the change of scene made up for the tedious work. Nowadays, finding one job is hard enough, and a history of leaving jobs 'because I was bored' is unlikely to commend you to employers faced with dozens of young would-be workers.

That is why it is important for your future wellbeing to find out what your prospects will be after the initial period of learning your way about and performing routine or uninteresting tasks. For, while it is true that few jobs are without an element of boredom and drudgery, and that work is only part of your life, you might as well have as interesting and rewarding a time as possible while earning a living.

# Where to look for a job

Now you've thought about various possible places where you could work, how do you tell whether there are any vacancies there?

## The careers office

Before you leave school you will most likely be introduced to the local careers office, run by the local education authority. The main functions of the careers service are:

- to work with careers and guidance teachers in schools and colleges to help you while you are still studying, and to provide you and your parents with information on educational, employment and training opportunities;
- to give you continuing guidance about work so that you can reach informed and realistic decisions;
- to help you find suitable training and employment;
- to help employers recruit suitable staff;
- to provide information about schemes which might be of use to you;
- to make links between industry and education services in each local area.

In addition, careers officers are professionally trained vocational guidance specialists who can work with you if you want to try for A and AS levels, GNVQs and higher education; if you want advice or training; if you are unemployed; or if you are physically or mentally handicapped.

When you are ready to leave school, whether for college or for a job, a visit to the careers office may prove well worthwhile, although it is no guarantee that your problems will be sorted out. Your personal history and preferences will be recorded, you will be interviewed by the careers officer and he or she will start thinking about ways to help you. If possible, he or she will immediately steer you towards any likely-looking vacancies; if not, regular contact with the office will ensure that you are kept in mind when new vacancies are notified to them. The officer will get to know you and may become more useful to you as time goes on, if you persevere. Sometimes young people report that the officers are somewhat depressing and hasty at first, but this may be due to a rush of school-leavers, or to the fact that you want what they can't provide. They are doing tricky work: one minute they are trying to find out what makes you tick and the next they are acting as recruiting agent for a local employer. They don't always find the right match, but they have to keep trying, like you do.

## Jobcentres

The government runs a nationwide employment-finding service with offices in most large towns called jobcentres – usually these have shop fronts on busy streets. Display boards carry details of jobs available in the district, and you may browse among the notices for as long as you like. If you see a job you like the look of, you tell the receptionist, who will help you further. You can visit the centre without having to talk to anyone, or you can go for in-depth interviews to help match you to vacancies available. Specialist staff are appointed to deal with young job-hunters and they can also give you details of the government training schemes that may be on offer locally. This is where you register for work, in order to claim benefit (see Chapter 8).

## Employment agencies

Privately-owned employment agencies exist in most areas. Their experienced staff try to match job applicants to vacancies obtained through personal contact with businesses of all sorts.

The service is free to job applicants, but employers pay a fee to the agency when they hire someone from that source. The agencies frequently specialise in one type of work – office and clerical, or nursing, for example.

Agencies may well handle jobs which are advertised elsewhere, but there may be advantages to you in applying through them. For instance, few people enjoy writing letters about themselves and often give a poor impression of their qualifications and interests. At an agency you should find a skilled interviewer who will encourage you to talk about yourself, and who will then pass on useful information about you to prospective employers. He or she will also tell you more about the job than you can learn from published adverts and, through knowing the employers and the type of people they prefer, may give you hints about how to present yourself and what questions to ask.

## Newspapers, radio stations

A time-honoured way of finding a job is to answer an advertisement in a newspaper or magazine. Most jobs in the public sector in particular must be publicly advertised to ensure the right of everyone to apply for it; many private sector employers also prefer this system (rather than having to depend on word-of-mouth recruitment), which gives them the widest possible field of enquirers. The national and the local press carry news of jobs; positions requiring more qualifications and experience from the applicant usually – though not inevitably – tend to appear in the national papers. Specialist publications carry adverts for jobs in their own field, and most public libraries hold a cross section of such magazines. Local and regional newspapers have a broad range of vacancies and are the best source for school-leavers without particular qualifications or specialist interests.

## Friends and family connections

Last, but absolutely not least, one of the most effective ways of finding work is through friends or family. Don't be too shy to let everyone know you are looking for a job, or to use the connection that might be offered. If an employer is satisfied with the way one of your friends or relatives works, the fact that they refer you will stand you in good stead. The employer gets the recommendation of someone he or she already knows and trusts, and has fewer problems guessing about your likely capacities.

# Identification of potential jobs

In starting a job search, most people identify early a number which interest them. Their concern is the relative suitability of these alternatives and what practical approaches can be adopted in choosing between them. If you are one of those and you are satisfied with your short list, go to the following sections which will suggest how your alternatives might be compared.

More work will be needed if you do not have a satisfactory job list and you have not, at this stage, identified a number of jobs which you might like to do or have only come up with a few which, at first glance, seem unacceptable. If this is the case, you may like to try this approach.

Relax. Sit down, undistracted, with a pen and pad. Then:

1. Write down, as quickly as you can, all the jobs which have ever held any interest for you. Put them all down as they come to mind. Try to get down as many as possible. Do not evaluate their suitability or reject them. Concentrate on what you would like to do however outrageous it might seem to be.

2. Give each a score out of 10 for interest. The most interesting receive 10. Once again still do not reject any of them, however bizarre.

3. Take the top-scoring half dozen or so and consider why they would suit you – why the job would be good for you and why you would be good for the job. Think about and write down the positive attributes of each of them.

4. Repeat the process again the following day without referring to your previous list. Try to be as open minded as possible. Do

not attempt to reproduce yesterday's jobs; just re-do the activity as if you had not done it before.

5. Now combine the two short lists and give the highest priorities to any which may appear on both lists. This can now be your list for evaluation.

The process may not be successful at your first attempt. This is because we are immediately inclined to think why something is unacceptable rather than why it might be acceptable, and what might be its positive aspects. This is a hard habit to shake off. Keep trying and you should come up with some reasonable possibilities.

# Eliminating unsuitable jobs

You have a number of jobs that you think you might like to do. Before undertaking research to obtain detailed information about them, you should eliminate those jobs which are quickly found to be unsuitable by reference to the lists that you prepared above.

Pick one of the jobs. Take your list of the essential characteristics that you want from a job (considered in Chapter 4). Does the job satisfy these essential requirements? If it does not, then reject it. You may want to be a travel guide but if it does not provide the opportunity for, say, the long-term successful career you have determined that you need, then move on to your other alternatives. Repeat this check on each of your potential jobs.

Next, assess each job against your weaknesses. Does success in the job depend on proficiency in an area in which you are poor? It is no use pursuing a career in, say, journalism if you have poor verbal skills.

This process requires that you be reasonably tough on yourself. It is difficult to put aside a job which has an initial appeal to you. It is easy to argue for keeping it for further consideration. But remember that you prepared your lists for the very purpose of analysing job alternatives and when you devised these lists they were an honest assessment of your situation. Do not now change the benchmark because it does not fit with your sympathies.

# Researching your short-list

You should now have a number of jobs for further consideration. These may be in different industries or professions. You probably know a little about each of them but perhaps not as much as you would like given the importance of your decision. You can, and should, find out more about each through your local careers office.

If you want to learn about a particular job, say computer programming, and you do not know anyone in that job, then ask among your family and friends if they know anyone appropriate and whether they will introduce you to them. You may be surprised how helpful and generous with their time people can be when they are asked for advice which could assist you in your career. Take advantage of this. The people that you get to talk to may be able to provide something much more than careers literature – that is, the insight of someone working day-to-day in the industry. They might also provide some handy practical hints on how to go about getting a job in that industry should you decide later to do so. The people that you contact in this way may also be extremely helpful in the future should you want to do research on particular employers in their industries.

This process of seeking out and contacting people who can be useful to you is known as 'networking'. It will be a very valuable skill in your future working life irrespective of the type of job that you end up with. Success in your career relates very importantly to whom you know as much as what you know.

The outcome of your research should be that you are now able to prioritise your list and perhaps eliminate some of the alternatives. The next stage is to start your approach for specific positions.

# Chapter 6

# Getting the Best Available Job

You have developed a short list of acceptable jobs. In doing this you have focused on your personality and needs and what you want from your first job.

In the process of getting that first job, you must now concentrate on the needs of your potential employer and adopt an approach which will satisfy *his* needs as well as your own. This will require that you 'sell' what you have to offer – package and present yourself in the best possible light.

This approach will include how you should contact, phone and introduce yourself to potential employers and how you should prepare yourself and conduct yourself in the all-important interviews. It will provide some valuable hints which will make you stand out from the others competing with you for the job.

## The employer's angle

The first job is so personally important to the new applicant that he or she tends to concentrate on what the job offers. There may be a sense of being entitled to the job after all the effort that has gone into education and training and level of achievement in them. While this is understandable it is counterproductive. These attitudes must be balanced by considering the point of view of the employer. The employer is providing a job because he or she wants something done. The prime motivation is not to provide a start to your career or even to teach you new skills or expand on old ones. An employer recognises that he will have to provide training, but as a means to an end. To him you are basically an economic unit of production. Your selection, induction and training is a costly investment in the future level and quality of your output. He has a job specification (just as he will have a specification for a piece of machinery) and will evaluate job applicants for the best fit at the least cost.

What does the employer look for apart from an obvious capacity to do the job? He or she wants commitment. It takes a long time to recoup the cost of hiring and training and it is only then that the new employee becomes a profitable unit of production. The employer also wants you to fit into the organisation as easily and quietly as possible. He does not want problems in managing you. He wants you to match and enhance the image that he is trying to promote for himself and his group. He may be concerned with your ambitions but only to the extent that your striving to fulfil them is consistent with what he wants to achieve by using you. You may know what you want, but be assured that he knows very well what he wants and he has had a lot of practice in achieving it.

The decision of hiring a new employee is very important to the employer. Should you leave before you can make a valuable contribution, or should you not fit in and he has to fire you, then the decision to hire you in the first place will be seen as a bad decision and reflect badly on his management skills. If you fail, he fails. On the other hand, if you are successful he will be seen as successful. So he has a strong personal need to have you perform well. If he seems concerned that you develop in the job, it may be that he is concerned about his own image as much as holding an interest in your welfare.

The process of hiring you requires that the employer sells the job to you. He wants you to be motivated and committed, so will promote the job in a manner which will satisfy your aspirations and ambitions. To get what he wants, he will try to convince you that the job offers what you want. No job will be a perfect match for your needs. The prudent employer will point out those areas in which your needs are not met. However, when you consider the motivation of the employer you need to check for yourself that your principal requirements are met, however open and honest the employer may appear to be.

# Approaching potential employers

You have your short list of jobs. The next step, which is to find out more about each of these jobs, is to approach the organisations where these jobs are to be found. In the process of applying for jobs you will find out more about them and hopefully be able to choose between them and get the one you want.

Each potential job must be approached as if you really want it. While the employer recognises that you need to satisfy yourself that the job really suits you, he would not like to think that you are using him to decide between potential jobs. He will expect that you have made up your mind about what sort of job you want and that you are only trying to determine which organisation is the one for you. The best strategy is to assume, for each job that you apply for, that it will be the one that you will end up choosing.

Importantly, while doing this, you must remember that you are selling yourself. You need to make yourself as attractive as you can to your potential employer. Generally, you will be in competition with many others for the job that you are after. To get it you will need to present yourself as the most suitable of all the candidates. In this chapter there are some ideas which will help you, all based on the underlying approach that everything you do needs to be considered from the viewpoint of the employer. Every time you present yourself or information about yourself you should consider what it is that the employer wants and act accordingly. The employer does not care for you personally (at least not at this stage). He wants someone to help him achieve his objectives. The successful applicant will be the one who best demonstrates that he can do the most for the employer.

## What do you want?

Notwithstanding that you will need to orientate yourself to the requirements of the employer if you are to win the job, you still need to be quite clear about what you want for yourself. In the past, in periods of higher employment, this was not so important – you could experiment with different jobs while determining what sort of job you really wanted. Today this opportunity does not exist. More personal preparation is necessary to make sure that your initial choice is the correct one.

## How do you get to hear about available jobs?

It is inefficient just to sit back and wait to hear about a job, and then apply for it. Actively seek support from family and friends in searching jobs out. When someone says that they are prepared to assist you, make it easy for them by providing some general written information about yourself. A single, neatly typed page will do. After doing this you will need, however, to follow up on your helper who may need a gentle reminder. A subtle way of doing this is to call about a week after providing the initial data and ask the helper if he or she requires any further information.

You may not immediately identify a job by this process. But it is possible that many potential employers will put your information on file and recall it later when a job becomes available. The cost to them in advertising and weeding out applications is high and they will often consider the initial information that you have provided them with as a potential easy and cheap alternative.

If you have identified a firm or a group of organisations that you would like to work for, you should approach them directly. Find out who is responsible for hiring for the type of job you are after. This is done easily enough by asking the switchboard receptionist. Then write to this person, who may be in the company's personnel department, in a large company, requesting an interview. The letter should outline your qualifications and why you would like to work for the specific organisation (you will need to have done your research – see below). Follow up the letter with a telephone call to the person. You may not achieve an interview initially. After your telephone call send a note to the person thanking him or her for taking your call and asking them to keep you in mind should a future position become available. Ring again in about three weeks' time and follow up with another note. Keep the process going. So long as your communication demonstrates good manners and professionalism your persistence should not irritate. When a job eventually becomes available you will most likely be considered before, or as well as, general recruiting.

# Replying to an advertisement

If responding to a job advertisement by telephone, ask for the person or department you need, and if asked, give your name clearly. When you are sure you have the right person, make clear who you are, which job you are interested in, and where you saw it advertised; the organisation may have advertised several jobs in different places, so be specific. You may find it helpful to rehearse what you have to say with a friend or relative. If you feel very nervous or shy, make a note on paper of the points you want to get across.

Use your voice to advantage, make it sound as if you are smiling – without giggling nervously! Answer questions clearly, without long pauses and 'er, well, you know...'. Have a good reason ready for wanting this job; saying you like the pay and the hours is not the best way to make a good first impression. Try something more personal, perhaps: 'I've heard about your organisation, and having just left school, would like to start where the prospects are good,' or: 'I need a job, I think I can do what you are asking for, and I'd like the chance to show it.'

When you are asked to come in for an interview, you know you are over the first hurdle.

If the advert specifies a reply in writing or if you are approaching a possible employer directly, think carefully about the presentation of your letter and application. Sometimes you are asked simply to phone for a form, which you must then fill in; and this must be neatly completed. Typing or using a word processor is a useful skill, as all applications look better when typed neatly, and if employers have many to go through, they welcome those which are easier to read. If you can't type, or the employer particularly requests a handwritten application, make sure your efforts are clear and easy to read.

It is well worthwhile getting properly organised for job-hunting and making a proper file and personal information sheet for use on more than one occasion. In the file you keep copies of all the applications you have made, so that you can save time by adapting them for each new vacancy you aim for.

# Researching the organisation

Whichever way you come into contact with an organisation that you hope to get a job with, you must carry out research into the organisation. Firstly, you will need to determine if the organisation is the one you want to work for. Research may not do this on its own but it may provide enough information for you to decide not to work there. Secondly, you may gather information about the organisation which will help you in your job application, for example, the organisation may have a specific operation which corresponds to an aspect of your training or your interests.

Ideally, try to find someone who works for the organisation. You may not know anyone first-hand but by asking around you may find a friend-of-a-friend whom you can talk to. Such a personal insight into an organisation can be invaluable. You may obtain informal information not available in the organisation's publications. At very least you should be able to find out what publications are available and how to go about obtaining them. This in itself can save you a lot of time and bother.

If you cannot find someone who works there, or worked there, or who knows the organisation well, then the first step is the direct approach. Phone and find out what they have available for public information. There may be annual reports, brochures, marketing material or copies of newspaper articles. You can learn a great deal about an organisation from these sources. What you learn will probably stimulate other questions which you can ask when you get to the interview stage.

You can also learn about an organisation from the other organisations with which it has contacts. Competitors, firms that supply it, organisations that use the goods or services that it produces, may all be useful sources of information. Keep asking around and you will eventually find someone who is familiar with your target.

If the organisation is part of an identifiable industry, seek out the relevant industry publications. You may discover articles about your target. Whatever, you need to undertake industry research as well as researching the specific organisation. An organisation can not be understood without knowledge about the industry in which it operates.

The appropriate level of research depends on the sort of job that you are seeking. If you want secretarial work it may be enough to know that the employer is friendly and pays well. However if you seek a technically skilled job, say, you may want to assure yourself about the standard of technical expertise in the place. This would probably take more effort to obtain.

Research into an organisation continues throughout the job application process and for months after you start the job. Before starting the application interviews, your research should establish that there are no obvious reasons why you should not work there. Also, the research should provide you with sufficient information for you to demonstrate that you have done your homework and can ask intelligent questions during the interviews.

# Your CV

Curriculum vitae (CVs), résumés, information sheets, are all names for the document that you provide about yourself to your prospective employer. There are many books available on how these should be prepared to portray the job applicant in the best possible light, indeed there are firms that specifically provide this service. A CV should contain:

1. Personal information: address, age, marital status, etc.
2. Details of educational achievement.
3. Work history.
4. A little information on personal interests, hobbies, sports.

It should be clearly set out, typed and preferably bound in some fashion.

All this detailed information should be provided by way of attachments to a single one-page letter which should let the reader know briefly:

- why you are suitable for the job;
- why you want the job; and
- how the employer will benefit by employing you.

Think of the employer who probably has to wade through dozens of applications. He does not want to read volumes of detailed information. Your one-page summary should give him enough to take you to the interview stage without boring him with all the tedious detail in the attachments.

It is important that you follow up the CV with a phone call to the recipient. After introducing yourself you should confirm that he or she has received your information. Then you should ask if any additional data is needed. It probably will not be at this stage but at least you will have demonstrated personally that you are keen and eager. Any way that you can differentiate positively from the other applicants, the more likely you will be to get the job.

# The first interview

Now the selling really starts. You need to make yourself more attractive than the other applicants, but how? This depends on who is interviewing you.

The first interview is often not conducted by your prospective boss. It could be handled by a senior subordinate experienced in personnel matters or, in larger firms, by someone from the personnel department. He or she will mainly be interested in your ability to handle the tasks associated with your job and will obviously have a good idea about this from your CV. You will be questioned on various details in the CV to confirm what is already assumed – that you can probably handle the task. Your role is to assure the interviewer confidently of your abilities and attributes to meet the expectations of the job (but not with too much conceit).

The key points an interviewer is likely to concentrate upon are:

- your physical appearance and characteristics – dress, speech and manner;
- your past experience and achievements;
- your general intelligence and initiative;
- any special abilities and aptitudes you may have;
- your interests and leisure activities;
- your personality, disposition, and personal characteristics;
- your home background and domestic circumstances.

If you think about these areas before you go in, you should be able to answer questions promptly and easily, and feel more confident from the start.

The interviewer will also be interested in your ability to fit in with the organisation. This is more difficult for him or her to determine. It is also difficult for you because you do not know what stereotype he is comparing you to. The best approach is to follow him, to copy him. If he is friendly, be friendly. If he is serious, then be serious. While modelling your behaviour on his, play it just a little more conservatively. This will be seen as respectful. If he subconsciously assesses you as someone like him, he should judge you as being able to fit in.

You should be seen as enthusiastic about the job. One way of doing this is to make sure that you ask a few questions that demonstrate that you have done your research homework.

Do not be afraid to ask about pay, terms and conditions, etc. It is not the best time to do this at the end of the interview, so make sure that you have other questions ready to ask subsequently.

It is very important how you end the interview. The last impression that you give will strongly influence the memory that the interviewer holds of you. So prepare and practise your behaviour at the close. Smile, hold eye contact as you shake his hand. Make sure that you thank him for his time in seeing you. Stand as erect as you can and walk out confidently.

It is not a bad idea to prepare for the whole interview by a number of role plays. Ask a member of the family, a friend or a family friend, who has had some work experience in recruiting, to act the part of the interviewer that you are going to see. This can provide you with a close to real-life practice of the interview situation. If possible, repeat the role play with a few different people. This will give you some experience of what it is like and, hopefully, some confidence at handling yourself in the real interview.

You should also follow up after the initial interview immediately. Send a note – a handwritten one will do – thanking the interviewer for seeing you and briefly stating your eagerness for the job. Ask him to phone you if there is any more information about you that he wants. In addition, a telephone call follow-up may help to add weight to your application. It helps if you can come up with some data about yourself, in favour of your application, which you overlooked at the interview. Or, ask a relevant and important question that you forgot to ask at the interview. Of course you can overdo this follow-up strategy, but what is suggested should not irritate most interviewers who will interpret your behaviour as encouraging enthusiasm to impress and to get the job.

# The second appointment

Your name has been placed on a short list for consideration for the job (it may be a list of one). If you have not met your potential boss during the first interview, or if he did not conduct it himself, you will get to deal with him face to face now. It is usually after the second interview that the decision to employ an applicant is made.

Your future boss will have spoken to the first interviewer. He also, of course, will want to know that you can carry out the tasks and that you will fit into the organisation. The first interviewer will have reported to him on these points and you can suspect that he will have a few questions of his own. What he will be after is an estimation of how well he can work with you. This generally boils down to how well he likes you. This potential boss, in some expectation that you might be working with him, will also want you to like him as well, so this interview should generally not be as tense as the first. (There are a very few characters who like to go hard on applicants, particularly if they think that an ability to be tough is an important part of the job.)

There are a few standard questions that you can expect and should prepare for. These are of the following type:

- Why do you think you will be good for the job?
- What are your shortcomings for the job?
- How hard are you prepared to work?
- What are your strengths and weaknesses?
- Why do you want to work for this company?
- How well do you get on with people?
- Can you be discreet?
- What do you dislike about the job?
- How much money do you want?

These types of questions are considered by some interviewers as somehow clever and revealing because they are aimed at putting you mildly on the spot. Prepare your answers honestly. Your confidence in giving them will probably count more than their content.

The second interview is also the time for you to ask any questions that you may still have. This is very important. Your potential boss may be offering you a job with the money, status, possibility for career advancement, etc, but you are offering him or her something just as important. This includes your time, effort and talents and might also involve your loyalty, trust and dependence. So, ask for whatever information you need but, of course, do not give the impression that you have in any way lost your enthusiasm for the job.

One of the questions you should ask is when should you expect an answer to your application. This is a perfectly fair request, so it will not seem pushy, but it is a good idea to follow it with a statement that you are available to provide any more information that may be required or for another interview if needed.

The way in which you conduct yourself at the close of this interview is also very important. You should be friendly, open and confident. Smile and once again thank him/her/them for the opportunity to apply for the job and the time they have taken in the interview. Leave with energy and poise. Some people suggest that you should end by asking for the job. This is only appropriate for jobs which require a certain amount of aggressiveness. Generally by your attitude, your questions and your responses to their questions, you should have made your enthusiasm for the job clear without having to ask for it.

Interviews have a second important function which you should bear in mind. While the prime purpose is obviously to choose a candidate for a job, the secondary purpose is for you as the candidate to see whether the job will suit you. This is important when full details were not made available in advertisements or preliminary charts, or if the setting of the job and your future colleagues are particularly critical to you. If you don't think you are going to be happy in a job after your interview and after you had the opportunity of asking questions, you should say so firmly to avoid wasting any further time all round. Despite the difficulty of the job market, other openings come up all the time, and if you are really uneasy about a particular position, give yourself another chance somewhere else.

# Making your choice

If you have not done so by now, you will have to decide whether the job really suits you. You have your list of what you are looking for in an ideal job. Compare it with the job that is being offered to you. It is very unlikely that this job is a perfect match. In fact, no job will ever be perfect. But make sure it has the main, important attributes that you are looking for and be prepared to compromise on the less important ones.

You also have your list of personal strengths and weaknesses. See how these compare with what is expected of you. Although a compromise may be needed, you should make sure that your major weaknesses will not be too obvious when you have to carry out your tasks.

Often it will not be clear to you whether the job is what you are after. It is a very emotional decision which will have an enormous impact on your life and it is a hard one to make. Talk to your friends and family about it. Not being so closely involved they may be able to see things more clearly and give you a different perspective which may help.

However, the decision is ultimately yours. Whichever way you decide and irrespective of what subsequently happens, once you have made the decision convince yourself that you have made the correct one. These decisions have a knack of turning out to be for the good. Do not feel bad if you decide not to go ahead. A new door opens for every one that closes. The next job that you apply for might be much more to your liking.

If you are offered the job and accept it, you should write a personal thank you note to your new boss and anyone else who interviewed you. But first, make sure you know all about the conditions of work: how much you are going to be paid, what your required working hours are, whether you may have to do overtime and what the rates are. Find out about your holiday and any other entitlements, and whether you are contributing to any pension scheme. If your employer is very small, check that he or she knows all about his or her contribution to your national insurance.

If you decide not to go ahead with the job ring your would-be boss and let him know your reasons. Thank him for his time. Follow this up with a letter repeating your reasons and appreciation. There is an outside chance that he may wish to, and is capable of, changing the structure of the job to suit your requirements. There is also an outside chance that you may come across him again one day in your career or future job hunting. If you leave him with a good impression of you he will, hopefully, remember you favourably.

As soon as you start work, a contract of employment exists legally. Normally it is written – it might be a letter, a document, or even a booklet – but it may also be verbal. In any case the employer *must* give you a written statement with the main terms and conditions of your employment. This must be given to you within two months of starting work and include:

- the names of both employer and employee;
- the starting date;
- pay rates and when you will be paid (weekly, monthly, etc);
- hours of work expected;
- holiday entitlement, if any;
- sick leave entitlement and sick pay, if any;
- pension and pension scheme;
- length of notice required by both employer and employee;
- a job title or brief description of job.

Make sure you put this statement in a safe place as it is a legal document and exists for your own protection, as well as that of your employer. The contents of it should come as no surprise to you, but you will need to be reminded of the terms if there is any dispute in the future.

# Handling rejection

You are not going to be offered every job that you seek or, even, every job that you want. The more you want the job the more likely it is that you will be disappointed or hurt if it is not offered to you. Firstly remember that it is not your fault that you did not get the job. Most probably you did not get the job because another applicant was better suited in some way than you. The attitude to adopt is as suggested above: that, in the long run, it is in your best interests that you did not get this particular job. Something else will come up which will be much better for you. You will be surprised how true this can be.

Treat the episode as a learning experience which will help you in your future search. The time has not been wasted. You have met new people, learned about an organisation and how it functions and practised selling yourself. You have been enriched by the whole affair.

# Chapter 7

# Keeping the Job

The first few months in your job are critical for your development in the organisation. How you perform and how you are perceived during this period will be the foundation on which you will build your career. Getting the job is only the first part. You cannot stop there, because many jobs are lost in the first three months. We all know of keen, new employees who have thrown themselves enthusiastically into their new jobs, worked hard and long, believed they were doing well, and all of a sudden they were dismissed. Why?

It is not generally because they have failed to carry out what was expected of them. Competent managers will, during the recruitment process, usually correctly assess the new person's ability to perform the actual tasks required. So why were these diligent people let go?

During the early days as a new employee you will be under close observation by your boss, peers and subordinates, whether you are aware of it or not. All have an interest, of course, in how well each new person can carry out his or her tasks. They are not just being nosy. Your contribution will affect them personally. For instance, if you are a fast worker, your peers will feel they must do better. They are also keenly interested in how well you fit in, whether you are the right type of person, whether your *image* is appropriate to the *culture* of the organisation.

It is fundamentally important that you are perceived in an acceptable light. If your image is wrong your advancement will be slow, or you could even be dismissed. It is not just how well you do your job that counts, but how well you are seen as doing your job, that is, your image.

If you develop a wrong image in the early days it is almost impossible to get rid of it. On the other hand, it is very difficult, during the first few months, to present a good image because, at that stage, you are unaware of the attitudes and values of the organisation and, therefore, what is expected of you.

The best strategy that the new employee can adopt is to keep a low profile. Later, when you know the organisation and have discovered the image you are supposed to have, you may then want to behave in a way that puts you in the best possible light.

Keeping a low profile does not mean making no impact at all. In fact, that is impossible. So the new employee must make some assumptions about what is acceptable, even welcomed, in all organisations. He or she should appear conscientious, loyal, hard-working, responsible, reliable, friendly, enthusiastic, and unpretentious. It is reasonable to assume that most organisations will find someone like this acceptable. On the other hand, it may become apparent to you that your particular organisation prefers someone who is, say, creatively outrageous. It is possible for you to move from your initial conservative position and adopt this new posture, but it would be impossible to go the other way.

With this low-profile image in mind, listed below are some suggested dos and don'ts which should help to extend your early days into a long and successful association with your employer.

# Dos and don'ts

## Do your job well

This is obvious, but with all this talk about image you must also remember that you still have to perform well the tasks that you have been employed to fulfil. Apply yourself, improve your skills, learn the practical aspects of your job and increase the quality and productivity of your output.

## Do not make out that you know it all

Whatever your prior training has been, it is very unlikely that it will have been enough for you to undertake your responsibilities successfully from the first. You will need to learn more. Any training that you may have had is likely to have been general. It will not be a total fit for the situation of the real world in which you will now find yourself. Be prepared for this. When you need help, ask for it. Your boss and new associates will understand that you will need to learn the ropes and will expect to have to spend time helping you to settle into the job and become productive.

## Do seek feedback

As well as requesting help in learning how to do your job, find out by asking others how well you are performing your job. Your boss should be giving you this feedback anyway. But your development, while important to him, may be a low priority. Or he may feel uncomfortable in being critical of your work. Make it clear that you want regular assessment of your output and that you will welcome it even if it is negative. Actively seek out this feedback. After all, this is how you will improve most speedily.

## Do not ask embarrassing questions

In the early stages, be careful in asking questions beyond the need to know how to carry out your specific responsibilities. Until you have proved yourself you are still basically an outsider and your information seeking may be looked upon suspiciously, particularly if you are asking about sensitive issues. Of course, it is appropriate for you to learn widely about your new organisation, but start with data that is unlikely to cause any concern. It is difficult to know early on what data might be sensitive. But certainly keep away from any questions which could imply any illegal, unethical, or distasteful practices; for example, do not question the company's attitude towards, say, tax avoidance. The angry response may be 'mind your own business' even if the company's practice is totally ethical. This is because the question at least implies that the company's practices could be other than totally ethical and this could be offensive. (It would also be offensive if the company's approach were other than totally ethical.) Also do not ask questions, directly or indirectly, about other people's private lives.

## Do smile

You cannot fail to impress if you are seen as friendly, bright, cheerful and unthreatening. The easiest way of doing this is simply to smile. Not a forced smile but an open joyous smile. It shows that you are confident and probably caring.

People who walk around frowning and seemingly not noticing those around them are considered arrogant, distant, stressed or unfriendly. Their personalities may be quite different from how they are perceived. Yet they are labelled negatively simply because they do not smile.

On the other hand, a ready infectious smile that warms the receiver will promote a very positive image of you and is one of the easiest ways to become liked.

## Do not whinge

No one likes a complainer. This is particularly true if you are still seen as an outsider. It irritates the listener because criticising fellow workers or aspects of the workplace is, in a way, the same as attacking the listener. This is so even when the complaint is valid.

No one likes a whinger. And once you are labelled as one it is almost impossible to live it down.

## Do be enthusiastic

You will positively impress others if you are enthusiastic. People find it an attractive trait. In the business environment it suggests that you will work hard and long to achieve your goals. It is an indicator of potential success. But it is more than that. Your enthusiasm can be an infectious motivator of others. Your commitment and dedication indicate that you are doing something that you believe in and value. This confirms to your fellow workers that they are also doing something worthwhile and makes them feel good.

## Do not act or dress conspicuously

During the early days when you are still looked on as an outsider, you should try to blend in. The most obvious way of showing conspicuous individuality (or your insensitivity to the organisation's values) is to dress differently from others in similar positions to yours. During your recruitment you will probably have had enough exposure to the organisation to know what will be required. When in doubt, be conservative. It is better to err on the conservative side than on the loud side where your difference will be far more noticed and unfavourably judged.

Do not think that the way your boss dresses is necessarily the way he would prefer you to dress. If he dresses very well he might be trying to demonstrate his superiority to his subordinates. If you try to match him he might see this as a particularly open challenge to his status. On the other hand, he may dress casually. But that does not necessarily mean that you should. He may see the freedom to dress as he pleases as something which he is entitled to because of his position. Dressing in the same way that he does may be seen as impudent on your part.

## Do learn and use people's names

You can make a very good impression on people by showing them that you have learned their names. It flatters them, particularly if they do not work in direct contact with you where, of course, it is expected that you know. If you use their names and they do not know yours, they will feel slightly embarrassed and find out who you are. It is a good way of making yourself known while still keeping a low profile. The combination of good manners and the use of their names will implant a positive initial impression with them.

## Do not become a victim of sexual harassment

Unfortunately, cases of sexual harassment do occur in some organisations. As a vulnerable new employee, there is a chance that some unscrupulous workmate, often in a position of authority, will try to take advantage of you. Keep your wits about you, and be wary of social advances that seem to be outside normal friendliness at work. It is important to make the distinction between innocent gestures of friendship and something that could make you feel uncomfortable or embarrassed at a later date. If you are tempted to form a relationship, bear in mind that an entanglement with someone from your workplace may well be frowned upon, if not prohibited, and you cannot rely on the other person's discretion.

## Do be predictable

You will no doubt wish to appear reliable and responsible. One of the ways of developing this image is to show that you have predictable work habits. Always work a little longer than you have to. This will quickly be noticed. Start a little early and work at least 15 minutes longer than normal finishing time. You will not be seen as a clock watcher. You will be considered conscientious and serious.

Let your boss know that you will be prepared to work late when necessary but request that you be given as much notice as possible.

If you are going to be personally uncontactable, say out of the office, let it be known where you are and why. The person wanting you will need a reason why you have inconvenienced him or her by being unavailable. If he does not get a reason and it happens a few times he will start to worry where you are. This can develop into a suspicion, perhaps becoming a complaint: 'he's never there when I want him'. When you become contactable again, get back to those who have been after you. It is an opportunity to demonstrate your consideration and also to dispel any lingering negative thoughts that may be held about you.

## Do get your objectives clear

It is imperative in the early stages of your new employment to establish what is wanted of you, how you will know if you are doing a good job, and when your performance will be assessed. In the terminology of business what you need are:

*Objectives.* These are concise statements of what you are supposed to achieve. Your boss may be disinclined to be specific. He may not wish to write them down. If this is the case, you write them down and get him to agree with them.

Ideally, objectives should be written in terms of output; that is, they should concentrate on what you produce rather than your intentions or activities in producing them.

*Measurement standards.* These describe how your objectives will be measured and how you can determine whether you have achieved them. If an objective cannot be easily measured it is not a good one because it allows for too much subjective interpretation.

## Do not phone your friends

One of the worst things you can do is to over-use the phone for social calls. You may wish to tell family and friends of your good fortune in getting your new job but you may not keep it for long if you do so during working hours. Remember that you want to project yourself as responsible, serious and hard working. Any behaviour which detracts from this should be avoided.

# More realities

You are expendable. Unless you live up to expectations, your viability is in doubt. Your boss, who probably hired you, will not only be disappointed if you fail to achieve what was targeted, he will be seen to have made a bad decision in having hired you and/or badly trained you. Rather than accept that responsibility, he will blame you and show that by sacking you.

On the other hand, your success will be appropriated. If you do well it will be due to your boss's astuteness in selecting you and his skill in training and managing you. If you put forward a clever idea it will be developed and made practical by him.

You are expendable, anyway. Even if you perform well, circumstances may change and take the job away from you. This may be unfair, but that is life.

You are still in competition. You competed successfully and achieved your aim of getting the job. It does not stop there. To keep it, to advance, you still need to compete – with others, with co-workers, your boss and yourself. And it will never stop.

You are an economic unit. You have a real role to play. You have to produce the goods. Your development and your productivity are not static. There will always be expectations of you beyond your existing level of competence. So you will always be expected to do more.

As part of this expectation constantly to do better, you will be watched to see if you are ambitious enough to learn more. There will be pressure on you to do courses, widen your experience and learn new skills. Lack of progress is stagnation, and stagnation is the same as incompetence, with the same result.

You will be required to be loyal. You will have to accept the ways that the firm goes about its business. You will be expected to agree to and to support and defend its decisions. Disagreement will be considered traitorous. And while loyalty will be demanded of you, it will not necessarily be returned. The needs of the organisation will come first and if that means forgetting your devoted contribution then that will be what happens. Do not expect gratitude. You may advance the interest of the organisation, help your fellows, do more than is asked of you, but do not think that this will be closely considered if the organisation wants to change your circumstances or even get rid of you.

# Relationships

A theme in this book is that it is not only how well you do your job which will get you ahead, but how well you are seen to be doing your job. Your image is just as important to your success as your technical skills.

'Poor image' is very robust. If you make a bad impression it is extremely hard to change it. Only time and repeated contrary evidence will alter others' views of you if you have made a mistake. As far as image is concerned, prevention is much better than cure. One insidious problem sometimes associated with a poor image may be a nickname, particularly if the nickname is derogatory. At first inspection a nickname may seem amusing or even affectionate. But it may still contain an unflattering message which is aired every time the nickname is used. Beware of the more sinister and long-term effects of the nickname. What is humorous today could be severely embarrassing in the future.

The most critical part of your image is how well you relate to other people within your job environment. Fostering, developing and maintaining different sorts of relationship are skills which every ambitious new employee should learn. There are some easily understood hints which if consistently practised will significantly improve the way in which you may be viewed by those around you.

# Personal conduct with colleagues

## Be well mannered

This is obvious yet it is so powerful that it needs to be stressed. Good manners indicate to others that you respect and value them. The courtesy and consideration that you express with good manners will bring you into high regard. The pleasantness that you offer will be returned to you when others respond with their own expressions of warmth and friendship.

And it is such an easy habit to acquire:

- 'Good morning';
- 'Thank you';
- 'Happy birthday'.

These are all examples of how you can demonstrate your concern and respect for, and good will to, those around you.

Every time you communicate with people you have the opportunity to impress them favourably by being well mannered. By self-observation and evaluation you can condition yourself to be constantly aware of this chance to reinforce a positive image of yourself.

Many communications in the workplace occur over the phone. It is unfortunate that many people give out such a bad image of themselves by the way they use the phone, particularly the way they answer it. You should greet phone callers in the same manner as you greet visitors. Give them attention. Give them an appropriate welcome. Introduce yourself. Let them know that you are there to help them in whatever it is they want from you: 'Good afternoon. This is Mary Smith. Can I help you?'

This will have a much more positive effect on the caller than just saying, 'Mary Smith'. It is more friendly and professional. Use this approach with all callers, not just customers. Your fellow employees deserve the same level of respect that is implied in properly answering the phone to outside callers.

## Be helpful

Helping others, as opposed to being uncooperative or indifferent, is the most positive way of favourably influencing people with whom you work. Helpfulness is a valuable gift that will assist others in getting what they want. In some circumstances your help could be fundamental to their adequately performing their job or growing in skills or image.

Hopefully, but not always, such helpfulness may be returned in the future and assist you in achieving your own tasks and improving your own image. Do not rely on it, however. Ingratitude is hurtful when it is unexpected. Also, do not offer your help with any stated or implied conditions attached. If people feel that they will be put in your debt they will resent your offer. They might accept it but they will always feel that you have taken advantage of them and this is no basis for a good relationship.

Helpfulness should not be extended at the cost of neglecting your own responsibilities and you must be prepared to say 'no' when spending the time to help could be bad for your own performance. But when you have time, or some special know-how you can provide easily, give your help generously.

The help that you offer others affords a solid base on which to build strong relationships with superiors, peers and especially subordinates and customers.

## Listen

Many people need to share their experiences, problems and joys. Lend a sympathetic or encouraging ear. They will appreciate your concern. Where possible respond with assistance.

Again, do not get trapped into this role when it will interrupt the performance of your own tasks. Make it clear, as nicely as you can, when you are not available to listen to them. Point out that you have your own more immediate problems. If necessary, set a time when you can talk to them later, perhaps after work if they really seem to need to talk to you.

It is not a good idea to be seen as someone who enjoys rumours or gossip. When someone wants to tell tales to you, do not offend by not listening. Just hear them out quietly and without comment. They will quickly realise that you are not interested in this type of communication. In a way this may be positive to your image. The rumour spreader will interpret this behaviour as showing respect for the person being talked about. So long as you do not offend the rumour teller by being seen to take the moral high ground, he may expect that when one day he is the person being spoken about to you, you will, similarly and publicly, demonstrate respect for him by paying no regard to the comments made about him.

## Accept advice

Others, however, will love to tell you what to do. They may offer advice with the best intentions or they might be patronising or seeking some advantage over you. It is very difficult to tell what might be their real motivation. When in doubt, assume that their intentions are straight. More often than not they will be. Listen and learn. You do not have to put their advice into effect. The important thing is not to be seen as rejecting it. Thank them for their thoughts and say that you will give it a great deal of favourable consideration. People will warm to you if you give the appropriate level of respect to their ideas. As they grow in the self-esteem promoted by your attention, your relationship with them will strengthen.

# Relationship with your boss

Your relationship with your immediate superior is critical to keeping your job and to your advancement. To a very significant degree he or she will determine your tasks, objectives, pay and progression. You will depend upon his evaluation of you for your image among his peers, recommendations for job enhancement and, perhaps, a reference for your next job. As well as applying the hints set down above, the following points specifically relate to your relationship with your boss.

Do not talk unfavourably about your boss or his actions to anyone. It will get around. It may very well get back to your boss, now or in the future. This is more likely to happen if someone wants to hurt you. And you can count on most people not liking you at some stage. (Of course, it reflects poorly on you with the one you tell it to whether it goes further or not. He might wonder what you could be saying about him behind his back.)

More positively, be alert to situations where you can advance or protect his interests. In particular, be aware of people seeking information from you which your boss may prefer that you do not make available. When asked about something, say that you are not sure what the answer is but that you will ask your boss and get back to him. It is unlikely you will ever be troubled by such people again.

# Salary reviews and performance appraisals

These are the two most stress-inducing, formally scheduled meetings that each employee has with his or her superior/s.

A salary review will determine what you will be paid for the next agreed period. It may include other than monetary entitlements.

A performance appraisal is more complex. It will review how you have been progressing and set down expectations on future targets and behaviour. Most likely, these will be done more frequently than salary reviews.

Each organisation deals with these reviews differently. Indeed, how they are handled tells you a lot about the organisation's culture, especially how it treats its employees.

It is better that these two be done separately. It is highly emotionally involving to discuss performance, when viewpoints tend to be very subjective. To include a determination of salary, based closely and immediately on what might have been a contentious exchange on performance, is asking for trouble. These will be discussed below as if they are handled separately.

## Salary review

Generally, salaries are set with view to what is being paid for a particular job in the market place. For each job there is a range along which your salary is likely to be set. In determining where you should be placed in this range consideration will usually be given to the following:

- experience;
- length of time in the job;
- level of training;
- length of time in the organisation;
- effort put into the job;
- relative productivity;
- performance; and
- organisational contribution.

As you see, performance is taken into account. Hopefully the level of performance applied will already have been determined at prior appraisals. While it is an important element in salary determination, it is only one of them.

'Organisational contribution' is what you do to help the functioning of the organisation beyond your actual job responsibilities. It may include consideration of your loyalty, willingness to help others, input to informal activities, etc.

The setting of salaries is not an exact science and no matter how hard an organisation tries to make it mechanical by having standardised procedures it will still involve many aspects which are subjective. It is unlikely that your boss will always assess your position on each of the relevant parameters in the same way you will, so disappointment is a frequent and an inherent outcome of the process.

You should approach your salary review with an opinion as to what you think you are worth. Your viewpoint will be considered by your boss to the extent that you have prepared it. (Your salary review is much more important to you than it is to your boss and he or she may have many such reviews to conduct in a short space of time. So you may be able to provide valuable input which he has not considered. Thoughtful preparation reflects your professionalism which is worth promoting at this sensitive time.)

Your self-evaluation might consider what other people in similar positions or levels of responsibilities are being paid within the organisation. But be very careful. What people get paid is extremely sensitive information. You may become aware of the salaries of others through the grapevine or because you have access to that information as part of your job. However, unless the person whose salary you are using as a reference has personally and directly informed you about it, do not use it. Although it may be relevant to your determination, the improper use of this information may cloud the issue and work against you.

External information may be helpful. You may have trained with people in similar positions to yours. This information may be helpful to your boss, who may not have access to such relevant data, particularly if there are few of your type of job in your organisation.

It is not usually your boss's objective to retain your services at the lowest possible amount that he can get away with. He is aware that unless you are paid a fair amount you may lose your motivation, and that your commitment and productivity could fall off. If you are badly paid you could seek employment elsewhere and the organisation could lose its investment in you and have the additional cost of replacing you. So, he is unlikely to risk a large loss by keeping your salary as low as he possibly can. However, knowing this you should not take advantage of it by squeezing the maximum amount out of him. Not only his pride but the necessity for internal consistency could result in his letting you go. The best manner to approach the salary review is to try to reach a result which is fair and satisfactory to both parties. In this light, you should not be surprised if your boss pays attention to your opinions and to any relevant external information that you supply to assist the process.

Advertisements for similar jobs may, or may not, be beneficial. While a job advertised may sound like yours, it may in reality be seeking someone with greater experience and you would not suit. You cannot be sure about its relevance until you apply for the job and it is offered to you.

The level of salary that you receive is important, but remember that it is only one of the rewards that you are obtaining from your job. There are many other important ones that may be provided in your particular workplace. These may include career development potential, and factors that you had not considered before, such as that your organisation is a good place to work, where there is a lot of mutual regard and respect, your co-workers are friends and you have fun, etc. So, when deliberating on your salary determination, take a wide view on the rewards that your organisation is offering you.

If you are still unhappy with what is proposed you may seek alternative employment. However, consider that your boss has carried out the process in good faith. With his experience and less emotional perspective, he might be right and you might be wrong. Also, consider how difficult it might be finding another position and how personally disruptive it might be to move. And the situation may be improved at the next salary review.

It is important that you take a note of any promises that are made to you during the review. For instance, your boss may offer you another review, outside the normal review timetable, conditional upon something happening, such as successfully completing a major project. With all the best intentions in the world your boss might make this offer only to forget it subsequently because it is so unusual. Or your boss could be replaced. Do a handwritten minute of the meeting and send it to your boss after the meeting asking him to confirm your understanding of his decisions. This could save painful confusion in the future.

## Performance appraisals

The objectives of performance appraisals should be to:

- commend and further encourage aspects which are well done;
- identify areas for training and/or support which might result in better productivity;
- identify aspects of behaviour which, when changed, would result in greater productivity; and
- set agreed objectives for the forthcoming period.

Unfortunately, in the process of appraising performance many appraisers feel that their primary task is to identify areas of poor performance and then derive objectives specifically aimed at improving these weaknesses. Aspects of performance which are being well carried out are often taken for granted and not recognised.

The performance appraisal is an essential ingredient in the management of each employee. Yet it is rarely done well. It often ends up a very disheartening experience for the employee and it can damage the relationship with his supervisor. Why is this so?

Often the boss finds it very difficult and stressful. He or she may find it hard to confront a subordinate with aspects of the subordinate's performance which are considered to be substandard. The boss might look upon it as particularly discomforting if he expects his subordinate to disagree and oppose him. This is clearly a problem for the boss which, if it exists, suggests that he, perhaps, should not be in management. This may be so, yet it is very common, so you should get used to dealing with it.

An extension of this problem is that the boss or supervisor has probably not been able to criticise or correct unsatisfactory performance or behaviour as, and when, it occurs during the period being appraised. As a result of this, issues are bottled up until the appraisal. A multitude of concerns, major and minor, may then come out all together, when it would have been much better for them to have been dealt with when they occurred. The result of this is that the positive objectives of the appraisal are lost in a rancorous debate about a range of subjects, of which many may be only of marginal impact on total performance.

A symptom of the boss's difficulty is inability to conduct the review on time. Of course, something urgent may arise which causes a postponement. But the resultant deferral is often handled very insensitively when one considers the extreme importance that the employee places on that particular meeting. Sometimes the boss may simply postpone the meeting because he or she is not prepared and has either not recognised its importance or is just not psychologically ready. In either of these cases the employee may be highly offended.

Many bosses handle these occasions as professionally as such important occasions demand. You should conduct yourself as professionally as you can, too. This means detailed preparation.

The preparation should have started at your last review (or when you began work, if you have not yet had your first review). It starts with having a very plain idea of what is expected of you. You should have your objectives written down with a clear notion of how you and your boss will know when, and to what extent, these have been accomplished. Unless you have agreed targets on what is required to be achieved, then you have no guidelines against which to assess your performance.

Your performance appraisal will be helped if you get feedback from your boss, during the period before the appraisal, of how you are going against your objectives. Your boss may arrange to have these informal assessment sessions himself. Often, however, with the best intentions, he might forego them when focusing on more urgent priorities. The best thing that you can do is to ask for the sessions yourself and be prepared to schedule them for a convenient time for your boss. Make it hard for him to deny you this helpful feedback. Holding these sessions regularly will have the following powerful benefits:

- You will receive information which will enable you to change your behaviour before the formal assessment which will be entered in your record.
- You will gain experience in dealing with potentially contentious issues about your performance with the person who is likely to carry out the formal review of your performance at the end of the period.
- These experiences should develop your relationship with your boss and should make the eventual meeting much less stressful for both of you (particularly if you have been able to get favourable feedback during the period and have been able to act on any negative feedback).

- Diminishing the stress in that meeting should allow more open communication and make it easier to talk about your future development.

In preparing for the actual meeting itself you should consider the following:

1. With reference to your objectives, list those in which you have done well. Put them in priority order. Your purpose here is to prove that you have achieved the core requirements of your job. This is a good way to start. At the worst you should be able to demonstrate a satisfactory performance.
2. For the objectives you have not achieved, or only partly achieved, provide an explanation. Remember that it is very rare that everyone achieves all his targets. You may have had more set for you than you could reasonably handle. Also, demands could have changed during the periods being appraised and some objectives have become redundant. So expect, as your boss no doubt will, that there will be some objectives that you will not achieve. If there were important targets that you did not get, make suggestions as to how these will more likely be achieved in the future.
3. Make general suggestions as to how your performance might be improved in the next period. This might include specific training that could assist you, or different ways of structuring your job. Naturally, where these changes are in the areas of your boss's responsibility you should make these suggestions very respectfully.
4. If you feel that you have the capacity to take on extra responsibilities in the forthcoming period, then say so and suggest what they might be. Your boss may have different plans for you but at least this will demonstrate that you are keen to increase your contribution.

You can write out a résumé of these points and give it to your boss ahead of the appraisal meeting. If you have already had ongoing mini-appraisals, your boss should not find any impertinence in this approach. Even if you have not had such sessions, it is unlikely that he will be offended. More likely, if you have prepared your thoughts well and provided a neat presentation of them, they will reflect favourably on the professionalism of your approach.

At the very worst your boss may reject your submissions, saying that all of them will come out during the appraisal itself. In that case you will still be excellently prepared.

In some companies you may be given a self-assessment form to fill in yourself as an *aide-mémoire* – it does not have to be shown to whoever is conducting the appraisals.

When the actual session arrives you must keep yourself under control. Keep on top of your emotions. Concentrate on facts. Refer to specific instances when it is necessary to give examples. Record the decisions that are made. Prepare a written minute of the proceedings for subsequent verification by your boss.

The performance appraisal is an opportunity for you to influence your development. Be clear on what you want from it, prepare painstakingly, and practise in your own mind how you will react whichever way the interview goes.

## Salary reviews and performance appraisals together

It is much less favourable for the employee when performance appraisals are not done or when they are done only as an input to determining salaries, which is what usually happens when they are combined as performance-related pay reviews. Development takes second place because historic performance is analysed as the principal determinant of salary.

Many organisations do it this way. They see the benefit to them as efficiency. They can kill two birds with one stone. Unless the manager is particularly skilled, this approach is likely to achieve less than when they are handled separately.

There is not a great deal that you can do to redeem the situation. Prepare as set out above. If possible, get rid of the salary question early. This should leave time for considerations for the future, such as your objectives and their measurement, training requirements, career issues, etc.

Some bosses identify areas of poor performance and then dwell on them. They do this, perhaps unconsciously, because it puts the employee in a position of impotence. Having to accept the criticism (if it is warranted – and the boss will always be able to find something to validly criticise if he sets his mind to it), the employee feels pressured to accept the boss's decision on salary levels. Certainly, he is in a weak position to argue. If you experience this there is not much you can do except to keep your cool and quietly bring attention to the other determinants of salary including, of course, your performance successes.

# Planning and self-management

Doing well in your job, whatever that means to you, is dependent on doing many things well. It requires that you, among other things:

- understand the culture of your organisation and act accordingly;
- develop a good image;
- cultivate a skill in developing relationships; and, of course,
- carry out your specific responsibilities well.

Most of the emphasis will be placed on the last point because that is the reason for which you were hired. But, if you are to do well and progress, you will need to carry out the other functions as well. This will not happen unless there is a great deal of planning and discipline in following it through, in other words, 'self-management'.

This process of self-management may be broken down into parts.

1. *Know what you want.* Analyse yourself. Develop an image in your mind of where you are going and what it is that you want to achieve. Imagine how it will feel when you have realised this ambition.

2. *Transfer this concept into a set of objectives.* What specifically is it that you must achieve in each facet of your job? Each objective needs to be written down. For each objective you will need to set out how you will know when it has been achieved and when you want it to be achieved by.
3. *Devise a plan.* For each objective specify what it is that you are going to do to reach it, that is, compile a list of activities which will result in the achievement of the objectives when they have been carried out.
4. *Periodic assessment.* The plan should identify a number of occasions when you will sit back and review your progress on each of your objectives. For some of them you will find that you are going well and on others you will be behind target. Your assessment should include assessment of why you have done better in some than in others. You should then adjust your plan for the next period to achieve a better balance in your progress. This review should revitalise your efforts and motivate you to continue to work on achieving your objectives.
5. *Evaluation.* Assuming that things go roughly to schedule throughout the planning period, at the end you should rigorously evaluate your performance and then repeat the whole process by redetermining where you want to go, redefining your objectives and setting out a new plan. By now you will have gained a lot of experience at self-management and should be able to devise a more realistic and achievable plan. Presumably you will also be able to see how far you have come and how beneficial this process has been for your development.

While this revamping of the plan should take place, as scheduled, at the end of the planning period, sometimes circumstances will change so dramatically that you will need to scrap the original plan and devise a new one earlier than anticipated. Should this happen be sure not to forego the evaluation of your performance against the old plan. The temptation is to concentrate on the future because the past is over. But it is more honest to yourself, and more beneficial to the development of your planning and self-management skills, to continue to evaluate your prior performance rigorously.

This concept of following a process of setting objectives, developing a plan, then reviewing progress and finally repeating the process all over again is an important one. Achievement is an end point of an intellectual process. It is not gained by luck or even effort, although these may often be a factor. 'Doing well' is something which comes from thinking, learning and, in particular, planning and self-management.

# Chapter 8

# Money Matters

If you have not done vacation work or a Saturday job, you may now need to consider money management seriously for the first time. A weekly or monthly budget will help you to organise your finances.

## Conditions of service

### How are you paid?

Whatever your reasons for taking a job, and however much you like it, there is no doubt that being paid is a great satisfaction! When you accept the job, you will no doubt have assured yourself of the rate of pay, and if you are wise, you will also have established how payment is made. This can be in a variety of ways and at different intervals. If what the employer offers doesn't suit you, alterations can sometimes be made. Different types of work are subject to different pay methods too – so, for instance, people who work in some parts of the car, or dock or clothing industries are used to being paid *piece rates*, that is being paid for the amount of work accomplished in a given period of time, rather than for the amount of time put in over a regular period. This work may differ from *casual* labour in that (in times of normal economic productivity) there is plenty of work and, although workers are on piece rates and without long-term security, the same people are regularly hired for the same work. On the other hand, casual labour involves working, perhaps seasonally (eg in tourism) or periodically, depending on the job in hand (on a building site, until completion, for example). Here you are paid regularly, but only until the job is concluded. Then you are 'paid off', and must seek work elsewhere.

Other non-regular methods of pay involve *freelance* work of many kinds, where you are paid for a particular job done – perhaps you sell an article, a drawing or a photograph to a magazine; or you are employed to help with the costumes or the cameras or the acting for one film or give financial or management advice as a consultant. This may sound, and frequently is, a somewhat hit-and-miss way of earning a living. But some people actively prefer the independence of working in this way. Indeed, over 10 per cent of the British working population is freelance or *self-employed*.

However, the vast majority of the working population are paid on some kind of a regular basis, as *waged* or *salaried* employees, receiving a weekly or monthly sum. You need to know how often you'll get paid before you start, so that you can plan your budget. On a weekly basis, you will frequently be paid in cash; on a monthly basis, you will normally get a cheque, or the money will be paid straight into your bank or building society account. If you have regular payments to make, such as rent, or hire purchase, or electricity bills, you can arrange for the bank or building society to deduct them regularly for you, direct from your salary. The convenience and safety of a bank account, once you are earning, cannot be equalled and it is well worthwhile asking at a local branch, or post office giro bank centre, how they can help you.

## Payslip

Each time you are paid you will be notified of the fact with a payslip, or pay statement. This will set out your gross *basic* pay, that is what you have earned before any deductions, and will include details of *overtime* pay – the extra money you earned by working additional hours per week, especially at so-called unsocial times, for instance in the evening or at the weekend; if you are due any bonuses, that is extra one-off payments, perhaps for special efforts, or for Christmas, these will be notified also.

That's the good news. The statement will then also detail the *deductions* from your pay. Everyone must pay tax and national insurance contributions, and there may be other deductions, too. For instance, you may want, or be required, to join a company pension scheme, paying a little money each week or month towards a retirement pension (if you leave the firm, a lump sum is returned to you), or your trade union subscription may be deducted from your pay if you agree. The final figure you end up with will be your *net* pay – the amount you will be able to spend.

## National insurance and tax

If you are self-employed you must arrange to pay your own national insurance contributions and tax levies, but otherwise your employer will work out the amounts you are due to pay, deduct them and pay them on your behalf.

You are allowed to earn a certain amount of money without paying tax on it, and if you have dependants, are disabled in any way, or are paying interest on a house mortgage, you are entitled to various further allowances. The service concerned with taxes is the Inland Revenue and, if you have any queries about your personal position, you should either ask your employer to let you know which office and person deals with your affairs, or ring your nearest office for advice. You will find it in the telephone book, under 'Inland Revenue, Taxes – Inspector of'.

The tax year does not follow the ordinary calendar year – but what is called the 'financial' year. It begins on April 6 one year and ends on April 5 the next.

You pay income tax to help towards the cost of services we all receive in this country. A few examples are the National Health Service, national defence, some social security benefits, education and road building.

The system is designed so that, as you start to earn more money, you will also pay more tax. You will normally pay tax on all kinds of earnings declared to the Inland Revenue, including tips, bonuses and part-time work. If you have any savings invested, income from these will usually be taxed, but the tax is often deducted at source. Some social security benefits are taxed but others are not. For example, unemployment benefit and income support are taxable, but child benefit, the sum you receive for each child you have, is not. The cost of tools or special clothing which you need at work can sometimes be claimed against tax if they are not provided by your employer. But you cannot claim for your national insurance contributions (see below) or for the cost of travel to and from work.

You usually start to pay tax when you start your first job. If you go straight to work from school your employer will give you a simple form. You sign it to confirm that this is your first regular job since leaving school and he will send the form to the tax office to tell them that you have started.

Your employer will also give you a coding claim form. This may look more difficult because it has to be used by other people, some of whom have more complicated tax affairs than yours will be at first. If you have other income, as well as the earnings from your new job, or you want to claim any allowances, you will need to contact your tax office.

If you have claimed unemployment benefit (see below) before starting work, your employer will have to treat you as though you were coming from another job.

## How is the tax worked out?

Your first employer will give you a PAYE code. PAYE stands for 'Pay As You Earn'. This means simply that you pay your tax as you are paid for your work. The code will be based on the single person's allowance (assuming you are single). If you use the coding claim form your PAYE code may have to be changed. The tax office will work out what extra allowances or income to take into account; they will send you a new code and show how it was calculated, and they will send it to your employer who will use it to tax your pay.

Your PAYE code represents your tax-free pay for the year. Your employer will use this code with 'tax tables' which spread your tax-free pay between the number of paydays in the tax year, 52 if you are paid weekly or 12 if you are paid monthly. On each payday, the tables show the right amount of tax-free pay to be subtracted from your earnings and you only owe tax on what is left.

If for any reason you are not paid for a while, the tax-free pay for those weeks builds up until it can be subtracted from your earnings on a later payday. If your earnings are less than your tax-free pay at any time, then, of course, you do not owe any tax.

If you claimed unemployment benefit before starting work, you will get a form 'P 45' from your benefit office to give to your employer. It will tell your employer what code to use for you. Until it is received you will be taxed on 'emergency code', which may mean a refund at the end of the tax year.

When you leave a job, it is important to ask your employer for the P 45. This is a leaving certificate which shows your PAYE code, your total earnings and how much tax you have paid since the start of the tax year. Remember to give this form to your new employer so that he can deduct the right amount of tax from your pay. If you do not give your new employer a P 45, again you may well pay more tax than necessary as the emergency code will be used. If you cannot find your P 45, you must fill in a coding claim form, and send it to the tax office, who will re-code you.

If you leave one job and have to claim unemployment benefit, you should give your P 45, which you normally get on leaving a job for whatever reason, to the benefit office. When you sign off, they will send you a new P 45 for your new employer.

If you take a holiday job while at college, say, and it seems likely that you will earn less spread over the whole of the tax year than the amount of the single person's allowance, tell your employer when you start. It may be possible for him or her to arrange with the tax office to pay you without deducting tax at all. In any event you will be due a refund if you do pay tax on this sort of amount.

At the end of the tax year your employer tells the tax office how much you have earned and how much tax you have paid. The tax office checks these figures with your PAYE code to see that the amount of tax paid is right.

If your personal circumstances change at any time, your code will need to be changed. For instance, you may get married, or you may receive extra income, such as interest from a bank account. Tell the tax office at once. Otherwise you may pay too much tax or, much worse, be faced later with a bill for tax you have not paid. Never be tempted to avoid telling the Inland Revenue about all your earnings; of course you may get away with it, but if you don't, the penalties for tax avoidance are severe.

## National insurance

The social security system in this country is designed to ensure that people whether in work or not, old or young, sick, disabled, or healthy, do not suffer from basic poverty. The system works through a national insurance scheme whereby those in work, and those employing staff pay regular contributions into a national fund. The fund is further expanded from the general taxation revenue. Three main kinds of benefits and services are offered through the social security system.

The first is national insurance benefits, to which you are entitled only if you have made the appropriate contributions.

The second group is non-contributory benefits, which means they may be paid to people who have not contributed to the fund (child benefits paid to anyone bringing up a child or children are the best-known example of this).

The third group is means-tested benefits which may be paid to individuals and families who have very low or no incomes. Here, people must explain to officials of the Department of Social Security, at the social security office, how much money is coming into their home, and their benefits are calculated accordingly.

## National insurance – related benefits

From the age of 16 you have to pay contributions if you work for an employer and if your wages are at least the 'weekly lower earnings limit' (this figure is adjusted each financial year). You must also pay if you are self-employed, but you are not then eligible for unemployment benefit.

Employers pay contributions for each person working for them as well, and you should ensure that this is being done on your behalf or you may be in trouble claiming benefits later if contributions are not up to date.

At around the time you leave school, you should be sent a card which shows your national insurance number. Check it and make sure the facts on it are right; if so, keep it in a safe place. You will always need your national insurance number when you start a new job, throughout your life. You risk losing benefit if your contributions can't be recorded. If there are problems, take the card to your local social security office – you can find the address in the telephone book under 'Social Security, Department of'. If you are over school-leaving age and no card has been sent, enquire at the office. The benefits to which regular payment into the national insurance scheme entitle you include sickness and invalidity, maternity, pension – and unemployment benefit.

*Jobseeker's Allowance* is payable when you are out of work, if you are capable of and available for work and have paid enough national insurance contributions or have income and capital below certain levels. You must normally be aged over 18 and out of work or working less than 16 hours a week.

It may give you some consolation when paying your national insurance and tax contributions to know that, if you become unemployed (and that is often far from being your own fault), the system then works in your favour. Also, if you have friends who have been unsuccessful in finding a job, they benefit in some sense from your, and other people's, comparative good fortune.

## Holidays

There is no law concerning holiday entitlement, except in respect of bank holidays, and individual agreements are negotiated by employers and staff, either personally or collectively.

## Other employer responsibilities

Apart from providing you with a written contract of employment covering all essential details, and with a weekly or monthly written pay statement, your employer also undertakes to take reasonable care of your personal safety, to pay the agreed wage or salary, and not require unlawful acts of you.

## Your duties

On your side, you undertake to obey all lawful and reasonable orders, to comply with all safety regulations and company rules, to refrain from misconduct, and to use reasonable skill in your work.

Provided that both you and your employer abide reasonably by these regulations and duties, all should be well between you. If you feel that you are being used unfairly and that your employer is not fulfilling conditions undertaken, take advice before doing anything. Your union representative may be able to help, so might a Citizens' Advice Bureau or a Law Centre. But complaint without secure foundation will merely label you as a trouble-maker!

If you are dismissed for reasons other than your own misconduct, there are legal protections due to you and the following section outlines them in some detail. Because of the changing nature of industries, job security cannot be guaranteed and individuals need the maximum advantages if they find themselves in altered circumstances or even without work at all.

# Redundancy

If you are made redundant, that is you have been dismissed through no fault of your own, you are entitled to certain statutory or legal rights. But you also have these rights even if you volunteer for redundancy. It is important to establish that 'genuine' redundancy has taken place – that is, that you lost your job because it could no longer exist. If your job still exists because someone else is doing it, then you are not genuinely redundant; you can make a claim to an industrial tribunal in an attempt to prove that you have been unfairly dismissed.

An industrial tribunal is an informal court which decides on disputes arising between employees and employers over employment law. Most cases brought before industrial tribunals concern unfair dismissal. If you are involved in such a case, you will need advice in preparing a claim and in going to the tribunal. Your trade union, a Law Centre or Citizens' Advice Bureau should be able to help.

## Situations of redundancy

There are three basic situations in which redundancy may arise.

1. When the business *closes* or is *taken over*. This may be permanent, but redundancy also occurs if there is a temporary closedown, and you are laid off or put on short time (that is, you will be re-hired when work resumes). If a firm is taken over you will be redundant if the old or new boss sacks you. If you are kept on but the work you do is substantially different, you can also claim redundancy. If your work remains the same, you are not redundant, but make sure you keep your continuity of employment, which will be important for any future redundancy claim.
2. If your employer *moves* and you don't want to, you can be dismissed for refusing to move, and still have your redundancy rights. However, if your contract of employment requires you to move, you cannot claim redundancy.
3. If your employer finds there are *too many workers*, there may or may not be a situation of redundancy. If new technology replaces workers, if there is overstaffing and some workers are sacked, if your hours are drastically cut and you resign, if your *type* of work comes to an end, then these are usually redun-

dancy situations unless your contract of employment includes terms which permit your employer such practices.

If your employer offers you suitable alternative work and you refuse it unreasonably, then you *cannot* claim redundancy.


## Rights on redundancy

You are entitled to the following rights if you are made redundant:

- notice, or wages instead of notice;
- time off with pay to look for new work or re-training;
- written reasons for your dismissal;
- a redundancy payment and a statement of how it is calculated;
- if you have been made redundant unfairly, compensation or your job back;
- what is known as a 'protective award' if your employer has not consulted your union or representative (see page 112);
- if your employer goes out of business, a guarantee of certain debts owing to you.

*Notice or wages in lieu of notice.* As long as you have worked for a firm for four weeks you are entitled to a legal minimum of one week's notice. This increases to two weeks if you have worked continuously for the same firm for two years. After this it increases by one week for each year worked, up to a maximum of 12 years, when you will get 12 weeks' notice. If you are dismissed (and redundancy is a dismissal), then your employer must give you this period of notice or the equivalent in weeks' pay. However, you may be entitled to more, depending on the terms of your contract of employment.

*Time off.* You are entitled by law, if made redundant, to have paid time off to look for another job or to make arrangements for re-training. You can take your employer to an industrial tribunal if he does not let you have it.

*Written reasons for your dismissal.* When you are dismissed, whatever the circumstances, you have the right to be told the reasons for your dismissal in writing. If your employer refuses or if the reasons are inadequate or untrue, you can make a claim to an industrial tribunal within three months of being dismissed (made redundant) and you may be awarded two weeks' pay in compensation.

*Redundancy payment.* By law, you are entitled to redundancy payment if:

1. you are genuinely redundant (see p 105);
2. you have worked continuously for the same employer full time for at least two years;
3. you are over 20 – since you do not qualify for any of the time you worked when you were under 18.

Redundancy payment, then, is calculated according to your age, your period of continuous employment and your basic weekly pay *before* deductions of tax and insurance. You are also entitled to a statement of how it is calculated.

The redundancy calculations are worked out in the following way: for each full year you worked for the firm between 18 and 21 you get half a week's pay; for each full year you worked between 22 and 40 you get one week's pay. (So if, for example, you started work with a firm at 18 and are made redundant at 23 you will be owed three and a half weeks' pay.) After 40 years of age, the rate is one and a half weeks' pay (up to normal retirement age).

Again, if you do not get this payment, you may take your employer to an industrial tribunal.

Many employers offer much more generous schemes than this basic legal minimum to employees being made redundant or offered voluntary redundancy. Also, a strong union may greatly improve such terms (as well as preventing redundancies!).

## Unfair redundancy

In certain circumstances you may feel that you were unfairly selected for redundancy, for example when the employer has not followed an agreed procedure for deciding redundancy, such as 'last in, first out'. Also, if you have not been considered for alternative jobs, the employer may be shown by an industrial tribunal to have acted unfairly.

## Consultation

An employer who proposes to make redundant at least 20 employees within any period of 90 days is required to consult representatives of the employees who may be affected. These representatives may be officials of a recognised trade union or employees elected by those who may be affected. The employer must disclose certain information to these representatives in writing, including the reasons for the redundancies, the numbers involved, the method of selection and the time by which the redundancies will be effective, should be discussed.

If this is not done the representatives, and in some cases you yourself, can go to the industrial tribunal and claim 'a protective award'. This is an award of so many days' pay for the workers affected, which is worked out according to how serious the failure to consult was. The more workers are made redundant, the longer the required consultation period. For example, for 20 to 99 workers at least 30 days and for over 100 workers, at least 90 days.

The fact that your representatives have gone to an industrial tribunal on this issue will not affect your claims for redundancy award or for unfair redundancy.

## Insolvency of your employer

If your employer goes out of business you can claim against the National Insurance money which will be paid to you by the Secretary of State for Trade and Industry where you are, in fact, dismissed.

You are entitled to:

- up to eight weeks' arrears of wages and up to six weeks' arrears of holiday pay (up to a limit);

- pay in lieu of statutory notice (up to a limit);
- basic award of 'unfair dismissal' compensation (equivalent to a redundancy award);
- redundancy pay;
- unpaid employer's contributions to your pension scheme.

For further information you can ring Freephone 0800 848489.

# Chapter 9

# Final Ideas

You cannot always achieve all your career objectives because often they will conflict with broader life objectives and values. You will need to decide upfront (and periodically reassess throughout your career) your position with respect to possible conflicts with the following:

*Family.* Will your career mean postponing a family, perhaps not having one at all? If you have a spouse and children, will your work responsibilities detract from spending the necessary time in sustaining and developing your relationship with them?

*Social life.* To what extent will you let your job interfere with your social life? Are you prepared to forego developing new friends and personal relationships in favour of your job opportunities?

*Friendships.* Close friendships need sustaining and will degenerate without having time devoted to them. Are you prepared to make this commitment if it detracts from your career opportunities?

*Where you live.* Are you prepared to change towns, cities, counties, even countries to further your career? How important is this and other aspects which make up your quality of life?

*Company.* Your present organisation may have given you your start and furthered your career. Co-workers may have grown to depend on you. Will you let a commitment to your company and associates stand in the way of your career advancement? Under what circumstances will it/won't it?

*Laws.* Under what circumstances, if any, will you be prepared to break the law to advance the interests of your organisation and yourself? You may not be prepared to overextend your parking time when visiting a customer.

*Ethical considerations.* How far will you go? Will you lie to sell your firm's products? Will you lie when breaking an appointment with someone that you want to put off? Will you undermine co-workers for your own advancement?

Conflicts will arise which must be resolved. Many will not be clear-cut and will be difficult to find a solution to. It is possible that these questions will be some of the most important in your life.

You should start thinking about these issues at the beginning of your career. Your decisions may determine the quality of your life and the way in which you will look back and evaluate it later.

# Fun

Work and career are serious issues. You will spend a great deal of time and effort in your work life. It will not only occupy most of your daylight hours but your emotions and aspirations, too. It will be interdependent with your family life and social life. It is precisely because it is so time consuming and important that you should enjoy it – not just the enjoyment of a job well done or the satisfaction of successful achievement, but the fun derived from continuous involvement with something that you really like doing.

It is much more than a romantic notion that we should seek enjoyment in our work. Obviously, we cannot all do something that we enjoy all the time. At some period in our careers we will find ourselves in positions that we do not like. Even in jobs that we basically like there will be aspects to them or periods which we do not like. But it is unhealthy to remain in situations where we are unhappy. After a period of time we will spiritually waste away and become ill. Work performance will fall off and it will affect our activities in the other parts of our lives. It is not worth whatever the rewards are that we are seeking to stay in a degrading situation like that.

More positively, having a job that you truly enjoy is a real treasure. It will raise your quality of life and its beneficial effects will flow over into the other areas of your life. It will add to the meaning and fulfilment of your existence. In a position like this you will find outstanding performance easy to achieve. Your enthusiasm will make light of hard work. You will be more creative and imaginative. Your positive attitude will impress others and you will be considered as a natural leader.

With this in mind, the potential for enjoyment is probably the most important characteristic that you should consider when evaluating your existing position or a potential one. Remuneration, career potential and professional development are important rewards that you may desire. However, unless you enjoy your job it is unlikely that you will be able to apply yourself successfully enough for long enough to obtain them. Being forced to stick in a position that you loathe is, perhaps, like being in prison. It might be tolerable but it definitely degrades you.

# Spare time

If you have reasonable luck (and never underestimate its importance!) you should be well placed to enjoy the different life which being at work opens to you. You can sort out your living arrangements, perhaps staying at home and contributing towards your keep, or finding lodgings, or a flat on your own or with others. You'll have to work out your basic expenses – board, lodging and so on – and desirable extras. And you'll find out how you prefer to use your spare time.

You may well find that, after the first excitement of being paid and starting to live your own life, you want to spend some of this spare time developing interests and skills which will stand you in good stead as the years go by. Indeed, an activity you have undertaken for fun and recreation may at some point in the future turn into a source of income for you. Over recent years, as many workers have been made redundant because of economic recession or because of the changing nature of the industry in which they had always worked, they have been able to put to profit other skills and interests which they had developed as hobbies. Together with even a modest redundancy payment plus, perhaps, a government grant to be used as an initial capital development, skills in model-making, cooking, knitting, engine repairing, painting and decorating, photography, coaching sports, and many others, have opened up different employment prospects – sometimes better and more satisfying ones – for people in their middle and later years.

# Other skills to learn

There are a number of general skills which, while not necessary in carrying out any particular job, may assist you greatly in your career and employability. These are distinct from the specific technical skills needed in your career and those allied skill/ knowledge areas which extend the applicability of your technical expertise more widely. An example of this allied type might be a knowledge of economics, which could broaden the outlook of an engineer in improving his understanding of some of the non-technical aspects of project decision-making.

Developing skills like typing, driving, or speaking a foreign language can be both interesting in itself, and useful in a job, as well as in your future personal life. Think of the jobs where typing is essential, or helpful: all kinds of office work, book-keeping, printing, journalism; in your private life, letters to your bank or landlord can be more easily recorded as well as read and you can help out as secretary to a community or sports centre.

## Typing, word-processing

Many jobs require extensive amounts of written communication. These include reports, memos and letters. When typing was a difficult and tedious task, it took up most of the day for the average secretary. Today, with the speed of correction and re-drafting offered by inexpensive word-processing, this aspect of the secretary/typist job is greatly diminishing. The secretary/typist position is disappearing and being upgraded to the role of personal assistant.

As a result of technological changes, typing is becoming much easier. It is certainly quicker than writing longhand. The old way of writing a report was to do it longhand, give it to a secretary to type, make longhand changes to a draft and then back to the secretary. It is obvious that, if the report writer could type, there could be a significant improvement in productivity. In many circumstances it could wipe out the need for the classical one-to-one secretarial support. One assistant might be able to supply a service to many.

In the past, extensive reports were most efficiently prepared when the first stage was done by dictation. Today, a report writer who is a reasonably proficient typist can usually type faster than he can dictate. He can certainly make corrections and alterations faster if he is doing the whole process himself. This is the case in large legal practices in the USA where the highest moneymaking lawyers produce their own reports.

Typing will be forced on those whose jobs require that they communicate via a computer. This is becoming more widespread with the evolution of the paperless office. Electronic memos and letters will soon be standard. Fax machines are being replaced by computer-based e-mail and modems. In this environment someone who cannot use his own computer efficiently because he cannot type adequately is out of place.

## Driving

Car driving, besides being a great personal convenience, is necessary for work as a chauffeur, taxi or minicab driver, courier, and in deliveries of all sorts. For bus driving you will have to take a public service licence, and for long-distance lorry work a heavy goods licence. An ordinary licence will open the way to training for these.

# Foreign languages

Foreign languages help with the travel industry and with translation and interpretation work of all kinds, as well as making your holidays more fun, if you travel abroad.

We are constantly advised of the growing importance of trade, not only with the European Union but also with the countries of SE Asia and the Pacific Rim. In doing business with people from these countries a knowledge of their language and understanding of their culture is a great competitive advantage. At the moment there is a shortage of people with these skills and consequently there is, and will be, many opportunities for those who have acquired them.

# Selling skills

Buying/selling is the process which goes on in every commercial exchange. In essence it is also the process which goes on in all human intercourse. For instance, in management, the effective manager does not order his subordinate to do something, he sells him the benefits which will apply to him if he does so. For an organisation member dealing externally with customers, clients and suppliers the process of interchange is clearly observed. It is necessary to understand that this process also occurs with other organisational members. Every time we want something from someone else, or want to influence them, or are ourselves approached by others, the process of exchange, of buying and selling is taking place.

Given the universal nature of the process and its fundamental importance in business, it is amazing that more specific attention is not devoted to it. Students are not taught about it. Surprisingly it is not a separate course in university economic and business courses.

Yet, as pointed out, we are selling all the time. It is the basis of all commercial relationships. It follows that the more proficient you are in carrying out the process the more likely you are to be successful in general. When selling is defined as not just the exchange of goods for money but more widely as the exchange of a benefit for something of value, then the force of the proposition is obvious.

Selling is a learned skill. Salesmen are not born. There are private training courses available and many books devoted to the subject. Learning about the subject is important if only because it promotes a sensitivity to many of the dynamics involved in the process.

## Communication skills

Selling requires identifying the needs, at various levels, that a person has, and then communicating concisely and clearly how you can satisfy those needs. Communication is a broader skill than selling in that it looks more at the total interaction and its quality rather than identifying a specific need.

This is an important subject. At a personal level, the knowledge and appreciation of communication skills may be very enriching in relationships with others. At an organisational level, communication is necessary for the transferral of information. Access to high quality and timely information is essential for an organisation's competitiveness. Well-developed communication skills will also provide a competitive advantage at a personal level.

Good communication means skills in the areas of listening, verbal and non-verbal communication and understanding. Knowledge and skill development in these can be achieved from a variety of sources, including business training agencies. Your company may offer you training courses in both selling and communication skills.

In our rapidly changing environment new technical skills are required and some of the old ones are disappearing. Our values and institutions are changing. What is not changing is the role and importance of communication between people. Those with high levels of skill in this area will always be valued.

## Public speaking

It is much easier to be an effective executive, manager or leader if you can speak fluently and confidently before an audience. Indeed, many people otherwise suited to positions of authority have failed because of their inability to impress when addressing a group.

Many of these people have a fear of standing up in front of others. They are afraid that their anxiety will result in a poor performance which may make them look foolish. Indeed, speaking before groups is one of the most common phobias. Generally people who feel like this believe that they were born this way and there is nothing that can be done about it.

Fortunately this is a misconception. Public speaking is a skill that can be acquired by almost anyone. As with learning any other skill, what is needed is an acceptance that it can be achieved and then become repeated practice.

Everyone admires the relaxed speaker who can effortlessly communicate his ideas and emotions. An executive with this skill is a significant way toward achieving success. As proposed earlier, success in a career is, to a very large extent, based on image and how you relate to others. Confident public speakers who communicate well with their audiences are respected and generally liked. The image that they promote is a great help to career advancement.

Training in public speaking and self-confidence is available from many sources, some courses being quite inexpensive and with all ages accepted.

## Speed reading

In just about every job we are required to read and assimilate enormous amounts of data. In fact, reading to keep up-to-date may be the largest consumer of 'non-productive time'.

Speed reading can significantly reduce the time spent in reading and improve comprehension. The time saved may then be devoted to output activities.

For those jobs or professions where continuous updating is essential, speed reading skills are almost mandatory if you want to operate at peak efficiency.

## Time management

As the promoters of time management courses point out, the greatest irreplaceable resource we have is time. Once spent it is gone forever.

Without being conscious of the overall impact, most of us have developed habits which result in considerable waste of time. Once identified, and with a disciplined approach to eliminating the bad habits, a surprising amount of time can be liberated and put to use, either as more productive time, more leisure time, or more of both.

It is simple and it seems too good to be true. Yet improved time management is a powerful skill in improving work output and quality of life.

## Learning the skill of learning

One thing is certain in our changing environment and that is that to progress we will all need to learn continuously throughout our lives. The days are gone when any knowledge, skill or profession was static. In fact, it is becoming increasingly more likely that people will totally change the nature of their jobs once, twice or even more times in their lifetime.

Learning is forced upon us so we should become good at it. As with every other skill, we will learn to learn best if we practise it. It is a good idea to set specific time-limited objectives for everything that we wish to achieve. This applies equally to learning. You could perhaps start by setting targets for learning in some of the skill areas set out above.

# Job-hunting again?

Work undertaken in a voluntary capacity, and which you may enjoy in itself, such as organising a youth club or football team, *can* also equip you for a different kind of paid employment, should the need or the inclination arise. Indeed, it may prove a real life-saver if you find that time is passing and you remain unemployed despite all your efforts or you lose your job for some reason and are job-hunting again. Time spent without paid employment doesn't have to be time wasted; you can use it to active and productive effect.

Once you have signed on you need not take all day to scan the job vacancies and make applications where appropriate. Despite the obvious problem of having no established framework for the use of your day, and the possibility that isolation, depression or boredom may set in, it is possible to work out your own patterns to keep busy and productive.

# Libraries

These are run by local authorities, and you can find out where they are from your local town hall or district authority offices. They have much to offer: daily newspapers to read for information and job advertisements; reference books in which you may make researches about companies or industries you would like to work for; material from local colleges detailing full-time, part-time or evening courses you might care to enrol for; records and cassettes you may borrow to listen to music; and of course books of all kinds for relaxation or study. Remember, too, if you are working, that libraries are open at lunchtime, on Saturdays and often late in the evening so that you can make use of them fully.

# Further education colleges and adult education institutes

As we have noted before, such establishments offer courses of various kinds and lengths, catering for all sorts of different needs.

Don't be misled into thinking that you must be available all day every day for years. There are numerous possibilities, ranging from full-time, two-year pre-degree courses to others requiring only two mornings a week for six weeks to learn, for example, how to run a play group for children under five. You can take GCSE in a subject you may not have been very good at, or which you couldn't fit into the school timetable, or you can take a full-time short course in bookkeeping, any of which may help you improve your career prospects.

In short, you can take vocational training courses, add to your skills, or just have fun.

## Leisure centres

Many such places, as well as tennis and squash courts, or swimming pools, are offering free or reduced entry to non-waged people. You can pass many healthy hours learning the crawl, or playing badminton, keeping yourself fit and your spirits up in the process.

## Community centres

In many city areas particularly affected by unemployment, special centres have been opened which welcome those without work. They offer useful advice, put on courses in response to special demands, arrange sporting and other recreational activity and organise short-term or part-time work. Keep your eyes open for notices of such places where you can meet people with the same dilemmas as yourself, share experiences and activities and keep up your morale.

## Youth service

Education authorities will have a youth service particularly concerned with the needs of people under 21. At the very least it ensures that sports and club facilities are available to a greater or lesser extent in any given area, and at best offers a wide range of services to young people. Find out where your local office is and see whether what is on offer might interest you or whether you might be able to use some of your free time to help (see voluntary work below).

## Museums and galleries

National and local authorities and private organisations of various types maintain collections of all sorts, most of which are open for public show some or all of the time. At school, visits to such institutions may have seemed boring or irrelevant to you. However, you may well find them of some interest now that you have more time to think, or are pursuing a hobby. They are most frequently open without charge and often have good quality, reasonably priced refreshment centres.

## Voluntary work

There is always plenty of unpaid, or voluntary, work. As with part-time paid work, if you are lucky enough to find any, it can be challenging and provide the chance to pick up new skills and experiences for future job applications.

As long as you remain available for full-time paid work, your Jobseeker's Allowance is not affected and it will usually be possible to combine such work with both job-hunting and any further study you may be engaged in.

Particularly if you are thinking about work in the caring services (with children or old people, in hospitals, prisons, or social services) you can find out through voluntary work in a variety of ways whether you like it, or are suited for it, and what the conditions and possibilities are, without being fully committed. Volunteers are needed to support full-time staff in many jobs, and some areas have local registers of such work which, although not paid, will not usually leave you out of pocket, as expenses are often covered.

There are many ways of applying for such work. Your local town or county hall will know of any registers maintained, and any general organisations such as Councils of Social Services, or Councils of Voluntary Organisations, which could direct you to places in need of help.

Taking advantage of all the possibilities there are for further education, development of skills and hobbies and participating in your community's life cannot but help you in your eventual employment.

Even if you don't seem to be doing quite what you had hoped for, these outside interests will help your personality develop, whatever your employment situation. You will build up skills, knowledge and experience of a real value to yourself and others. A busy, satisfying life depends on far more than paid work.

# Index